GUIDE TO

THE APPALACHIAN TRAIL
IN PENNSYLVANIA

D1431389

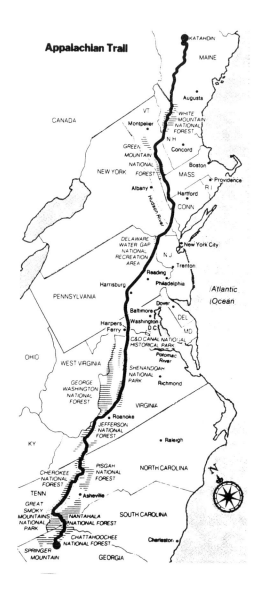

GUIDE TO

THE APPALACHIAN TRAIL
IN
PENNSYLVANIA

Number 5 of a Series

Wayne E. Gross

Editor

TENTH EDITION

KEYSTONE TRAILS ASSOCIATION
Cogan Station, PA

1998

Cover Photo: **View from Mt. Minsi, Delaware Water Gap**
Inside Cover
Photo: **View from Hawk Mountain**
                © Wayne Gross

ISBN: 1-889386-03-0

Dedicated to the memory of Helen Bickham, who would after Church pass on her copy of *Appalachian Trailway News* to this boy and helped inspire me to eventually view the wonders of the entire Trail by foot.

CONTENTS

DETAILED TRAIL DESCRIPTION 55

DISCLAIMER

Because of constantly changing conditions resulting from natural and other causes beyond the control and/or knowledge of persons and clubs maintaining the Appalachian Trail, Keystone Trails Association and all maintaining clubs and individuals, as well as all authors and contributors to this publication, must disclaim any liability whatsoever for the condition of the trail, occurrences on it, or the accuracy of any data or material set forth in this Trail Guide. This Trail Guide was prepared on the basis of the best knowledge available to the authors at the time of its publication, but readers are encouraged not to place undue reliance upon the continuing validity of the facts set forth herein; and it must be presumed that all persons using the Appalachian Trail and/or this Trail Guide do so at their own risk.

PREFACE

On a spring morning 50 years ago, a young man from Pennsylvania began a backpacking trip that would lead him from Georgia to Maine on a trail built by volunteers with vision and perseverance - The Appalachian Trail. Since Earl Shaffer's first solo one-season hike, many people have hiked its entire length and millions more have visited this treasured trail. From my days as a Boy Scout to my present days of following its white blazes, I know the efforts of the volunteers make the difference. To the many volunteers who make the Appalachian Trail what is today, on behalf of the millions who walk its path - Thanks!

This edition builds on the work of the previous editors and volunteers. The format parallels the work done by Maurice Forrester, the previous editor.

With this edition, new color maps of the trail are available for sections one through eight. Tom Scully's unending efforts to re-measure the trail and provide the most accurate maps available led to many revisions to both mileages and text. We have taken every effort for the guide to match the new color maps. The Potomac Appalachian Trail Club is updating their color maps for sections nine through fourteen. Dave Pierce provided many mileage and text revisions for those sections.

The sketches are the work of Robert Miller, a talented young man, who I first met in Scouting while producing a Where To Go Camping guide.

A new feature to the guide is the addition of "N to S" and "S to N" to the headers. This allows the hiker easier access to the section of preferred travel direction.

If corrections are found in the guide, please send them to the editor in care of Keystone Trails Association and to the local maintaining club for that section. Your help is appreciated.

May you have great adventures hiking the Appalachian Trail in the Keystone State as it unfolds in the following pages.

Wayne E. Gross
Cresco, PA
March, 1998

ACKNOWLEDGMENTS

The team of field editors, who perform the basic task of collecting the raw data from which the trail descriptions are built, represent the crucial linchpin, without which everything else would fall apart. This guidebook could not be produced without their help. Listed from north to south according to their Trail maintenance responsibilities, they are:

Wilmington Trail Club: Edward Sohl
Batona Hiking Club: Bette Irwin and Jo Ann Raine
Appalachian Mountain Club: William Steinmetz
Philadelphia Trail Club: Ed Kenna
Allentown Hiking Club: Mike Benyo
Blue Mountain Eagle Climbing Club: George
    Shollenberger
Brandywine Valley Outing Club: Patrick Markovic
Susquehanna A.T. Club: Jeff Buehler, Tom Scully,
    and Richard Tobias
York Hiking Club: Ron Gray
Mountain Club of Maryland: Paul Ives
Cumberland Valley A.T. Management Association:
    Craig Dunn and David Barr
Potomac A.T. Club, North Chapter: Elizabeth N.
    Johnston, Chris Firme, and David Pierce

Jean Aron, who chairs KTA's Maps and Guides Committee, was the source of advice and prodding to keep this project moving. Maurice Forrester, past-editor of the guidebook, provided this editor with advice and counsel. Tom Scully, through his unending hours of re-measuring the Trail in sections one through eight, provided countless measurement and text updates. David Pierce provided many measurement and text updates for sections nine through fourteen.

Brian King, Jeff Wynn, and Karen Lutz of the Appalachian Trail Conference staff provided assistance and comments.

Various agencies of Pennsylvania State Government provided a wealth of information that has been incorporated in this book. Roland Bergner of the Pennsylvania Game Commission; William R. Slippey of the Bureau of Forestry; and Ed Deaton, Chuck Trovel, and Gary K. Smith of the Bureau of State Parks all provided comments and advice.

The sketches are the work of Robert Miller and may not be copied or reused without his written permission. The photographs are the work of Wayne E. Gross.

This "two fingered" editor thanks Marlene Labar and Shirley Hearn for their help in typing the many revisions. He also thanks Jean Aron, the trail club representatives listed above, and Glen Lippincott for their proofreading efforts. The editor thanks the employees of RKR Hess Associates and Neil Frantz for answers to his computer questions.

Daniel McMaster of Sun Litho-Print, Inc. helped by directing this editor on how to prepare the document for publication.

A special thank you goes to Tom Scully for his work producing the new color maps for sections one through eight.

For my family's and friends' support and patience - Thank you.

Finally, thank you to all those who helped in a variety of ways but whose names I have failed to note here.

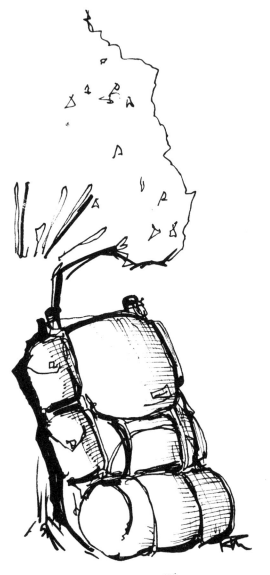

USING THE GUIDE

INTRODUCTION

The Guide is Number Five of a series of guidebooks describing the entire Appalachian Trail from Maine to Georgia. The other books in the series are listed on the back cover.

The book is organized with general and background material at the beginning. Included in this section is information on the history of the Appalachian Trail, the Appalachian Trail Conference, Keystone Trails Association, the nature of the Trail and land ownership in Pennsylvania, and general information for the assistance of hikers.

The bulk of the Guide, making up something more than three fourths of the total, consists of detailed trail description. The Trail in Pennsylvania is divided into 14 sections of varying lengths. Trail information is given for each section, with general material listed first, followed by detailed description in columnar format, North to South, then South to North.

In preparing this guidebook it has assumed that hikers will supply themselves with the Trail maps published by Keystone Trails Association, based on U.S. Geological Survey maps. For the Trail south of the Susquehanna River, the maps published by the Potomac Appalachian Trail Club may also be of interest to the hiker.

Most automobile road maps, as well as the Pennsylvania Official Transportation Map, show the route of the Appalachian Trail. These can be useful in determining the main highway crossings. A copy of the Official Pennsylvania Map can be obtained without charge by writing to: Pennsylvania Department of Transportation, Harrisburg, PA 17120.

1

ABBREVIATIONS

A.T.	Appalachian Trail
AHC	Allentown Hiking Club
AMC	Appalachian Mountain Club
ATC	Appalachian Trail Conference
BATONA	Batona Hiking Club
BMECC	Blue Mountain Eagle Climbing Club
BVOC	Brandywine Valley Outing Club
CVATMA	Cumberland Valley A.T. Management Association
ft.	foot/feet
KTA	Keystone Trails Association
MCM	Mountain Club of Maryland
mi.	mile(s)
NPS	National Park Service
PATC	Potomac Appalachian Trail Club
SATC	Susquehanna Appalachian Trail Club
USGS	U.S. Geological Survey
yd.	yard(s)
YHC	York Hiking Club

MILES TO KILOMETERS CONVERSION TABLE

	0.0	1.0	2.0	3.0	4.0
0.0	0.000	1.609	3.219	4.828	6.437
0.1	0.161	1.770	3.380	4.989	6.598
0.2	0.322	1.931	3.541	5.150	6.759
0.3	0.483	2.092	3.702	5.311	6.920
0.4	0.644	2.253	3.862	5.472	7.081
0.5	0.805	2.414	4.023	5.633	7.242
0.6	0.966	2.575	4.184	5.794	7.403
0.7	1.127	2.736	4.345	5.955	7.564
0.8	1.288	2.897	4.506	6.116	7.725
0.9	1.449	3.058	4.667	6.277	7.886

	5.0	6.0	7.0	8.0	9.0	10.0
0.0	8.047	9.656	11.266	12.875	14.484	16.094
0.1	8.208	9.817	11.426	13.036	14.645	16.254
0.2	8.369	9.978	11.587	13.197	14.806	16.415
0.3	8.530	10.139	11.748	13.358	14.967	16.576
0.4	8.691	10.300	11.909	13.519	15.128	16.737
0.5	8.851	10.461	12.070	13.680	15.289	16.898
0.6	9.012	10.622	12.231	13.840	15.450	17.059
0.7	9.173	19.783	12.392	14.001	15.611	17.220
0.8	9.334	10.944	12.553	14.162	15.772	17.381
0.9	9.495	11.105	12.714	14.323	15.933	17.542

EXAMPLE: To convert 7.4 miles to kilometers.

(1) Find the mile column labeled "7.0"

(2) Find the "tenth" row for that column labeled "0.4"

The intersection of the mile column and the tenth row will give you the conversion to kilometers, in this case, 11.909 km.

0.01 Miles = .0161 km.

KEYSTONE TRAILS ASSOCIATION

Keystone Trails Association (KTA) is a federation of organizations and individuals sharing a common interest in hiking opportunities in Pennsylvania and neighboring states. Since its founding in 1956, KTA has played a lead role in coordinating the activities of hiking clubs and other sympathetic outdoor groups in and around Pennsylvania. It keeps a watchful eye on actions of government at all levels that can have an impact on hiking or hiking trails. Through the quarterly *NEWSLETTER*, members are kept informed about hiking related activities in Pennsylvania and elsewhere.

One of KTA's major activities is the coordination of management and maintenance efforts relating to the Appalachian Trail in Pennsylvania. This coordination is conducted in close cooperation with the Appalachian Trail Conference, of which KTA is a member. The KTA Council and the various standing committees in turn provide the mechanism for coordination among the 12 A.T.-maintaining clubs responsible for Trail segments in Pennsylvania.

In addition to this guidebook and the map set intended to supplement it, KTA also publishes various other books and maps. These include *Pennsylvania Hiking Trails*, a summary guide to more than 2,000 miles of hiking trail in the Keystone State. Also published by KTA is *Guide to the Tuscarora and Link Trails* along with a series of maps for these two trails. Write to KTA for a copy of the current price list.

KTA also cooperated with the Pennsylvania Geologic Survey in the preparation and publication of Geology of the Appalachian Trail in Pennsylvania, which can be purchased from the Pennsylvania State Book Store, Department of General Services, 1825 Stanley Drive, Harrisburg, Pa. 17103; telephone 717/787-5109.

As the pressures of ever expanding development pose growing threats to the integrity of existing trails everywhere, it is important that hikers and their allies band together to guard against attacks, to keep informed, and to present a united front when necessary in the face of incursion. In Pennsylvania, KTA has provided a focus for hiker unity for over 40 years.

New members are always welcome. Dues for individuals are $9.00 per year, and include a subscription to the quarterly *NEWSLETTER*. An annual weekend membership meeting is held every fall, and an open meeting of the governing Council is held in the spring. A hiking program is sponsored at each weekend meeting. KTA also sponsors a hiking program consisting of several hiking weekends throughout the year. KTA's trail maintenance program includes a dozen Trail Care Weekends throughout the state. The KTA Trail Crew program, several week-long trail maintenance projects throughout the state each year, has been very successful.

To join, simply complete and mail the membership application found at the back of this book. If you belong to a group that is interested in affiliating with KTA, have your secretary or another officer get in touch with the KTA President.

KEYSTONE TRAILS ASSOCIATION
PO Box 251
Cogan Station, PA 17728-0251
http://www.reston.com/kta/KTA.html

THE APPALACHIAN TRAIL

The Appalachian Trail (A.T.) is a continuous, marked footpath extending along the crest of the Appalachian Mountain range for more than 2,100 miles from Katahdin, a granite monolith in the central Maine wilderness, south to Springer Mountain in Georgia.

The Trail traverses 14 states, primarily on public land. Virginia has the longest section with more than 546 miles, while West Virginia has the shortest, about 25 miles along the Virginia/West Virginia boundary, with a short swing into Harpers Ferry near the Maryland border. The highest elevation along the Trail is 6,643 feet at Clingmans Dome in the Great Smoky Mountains. The Trail's lowest elevation is only slightly above sea level west of its crossing of the Hudson River in New York.

TRAIL HISTORY

Credit for establishing the Trail belongs to three leaders and countless volunteers. The first Trail proposal to appear in print was an article by regional planner Benton MacKaye of Shirley, Massachusetts, entitled, "An Appalachian Trail, a Project in Regional Planning," in the October 1921 issue of the *Journal of the American Institute of Architects.* The author envisioned a footpath along the Appalachian ridgeline where urban people could walk in a natural setting.

MacKaye's challenge kindled considerable interest, but at the time most of the outdoor organizations able to participate in constructing such a trail were east of the Hudson River, where some existing trail systems could be incorporated into the proposed Appalachian Trail. The Appalachian Mountain Club (AMC) maintained an excellent series of trails in New England, but since most ran north and south, the Trail could not cross new Hampshire until the chain of huts built and operated by the AMC permitted an east-west alignment. In Vermont, the southern 100 miles of the Long Trail, then being developed in the Green Mountains, were connected to the White Mountains by the trails of the Dartmouth Outing Club (DOC).

It was in New York during 1923 that in the Harriman-Bear Mountain section of Palisades Interstate Park, the first section of the A.T. was opened by a number of area hiking clubs that had formed the New York-New Jersey Trail Conference.

The Appalachian Trail Conference (ATC) was formed in 1925 to stimulate greater interest in MacKaye's idea and to coordinate the clubs' work in choosing and building the route. The Conference remains a nonprofit educational organization of volunteers dedicated to maintaining, managing, and protecting the Appalachian Trail.

Although interest in the Trail spread to Pennsylvania and New England, little additional work was done until 1926, when Judge Arthur Perkins of Hartford, Connecticut, began persuading groups to locate and cut the footpath through the wilderness. His enthusiasm provided the momentum that carried the Trail idea forward.

In the southern states where there were few trails and fewer clubs, the "skyline" route followed by the A.T. was largely within national forests and parks. Subsequently, a number of clubs were formed in various locations throughout the region to take responsibility for the southern Trail.

Meanwhile, Judge Perkins had interested Myron H. Avery in the Trail. Avery, who chaired the ATC from 1931 to 1952, enlisted the aid and coordinated the work of hundreds of men and women who brought the Trail to its completion on August 14, 1937, when the ridge between Spaulding and Sugarloaf Mountains in Maine became the last section to be opened.

Following the completion of the Trail, the problem of maintaining its wilderness character became increasingly difficult, as highway encroachments, housing developments, and summer resorts caused more and more relocations.

In response to these threats, a plan was proposed by Edward B. Ballard at the eighth general meeting of the Appalachian Trail Conference to establish an "Appalachian Trailway." Under this plan an area on each side of the Trail would be set apart to safeguard the interests of those who travel on foot. Ballard's proposal was accepted by the Conference.

Measures taken to implement this long-range Appalachian Trail protection program culminated first in the execution on October 15, 1938, of an agreement between the National Park

Service and the U.S. Forest Service for the promotion of an Appalachian Trailway through the relevant national parks and forests for a distance extending one mile on each side of the Trail. Within this zone, no new parallel roads would be built and no other incompatible development would be allowed. In addition, no timber cutting would be permitted within 200 feet of the Trail. Similar agreements, creating a zone one quarter mile wide, were signed with the states through which the Trail passes.

Three decades of work battling encroachments followed, before Congress, in 1968, established a national system of trails, and designated as the initial components, the Appalachian Trail and the Pacific Crest Trail. The National Trails System Act directs the Secretary of the Interior, in consultation with the Secretary of Agriculture, to administer the Appalachian Trail primarily as a footpath and to protect the Trail against incompatible activities. Provision was also made for acquiring rights-of-way for the Trail both inside and outside the boundaries of federally administered areas.

In 1970, supplemental agreements among the National Park Service, the U.S. Forest Service, and the Appalachian Trail Conference established, under the act, the specific responsibilities of these organizations for the initial mapping, selection of rights-of-way, relocations, maintenance, development, acquisition of land, and protection of a permanent Trail. Agreements also were signed between the Park Service and the various states, encouraging each state to acquire and protect a right-of-way for the Trail outside federal land.

The slow progress of federal efforts and the lack of initiative by some states led congress in 1978 to amend the National Trails System Act. The amendment, known as The Appalachian Trail Bill, was signed by President Jimmy Carter on March 21, 1978. The new legislation emphasized the need for Trail protection through the acquisition of a corridor, and authorized $90 million for that purpose. As of the date of this publication, Trail protection was about 98% complete.

Additional Information. The Appalachian Trail Conference offers a variety of publications relating to the Appalachian Trail and its history. Write to the Conference at the address given below for a copy of the current publications list.

THE APPALACHIAN TRAIL CONFERENCE

The Appalachian Trail Conference (ATC) is a volunteer, nonprofit corporation dedicated to the maintenance and preservation of the Appalachian Trail. ATC coordinates the efforts of trail clubs, state and local governments, the National Park Service, and individuals in trail management and maintenance. The Conference publishes booklets of various types and guidebooks for many A.T. sections. Guide books for all sections (whether published by ATC or others) are available from the ATC office. In addition, the Conference supplies information on the construction and maintenance of hiking trails and general information on hiking and trail use.

The membership of the Conference is made up of organizations which maintain the Trail or contribute to the Trail project, individuals who in either personal or official capacity are responsible for the maintenance of sections of the Trail, and individual dues-paying members.

ATC membership includes a subscription to *Appalachian Trailway News*, published five times a year. The Conference also issues a bi-monthly newsletter, *The Register*, written primarily for Trail maintainers. Guidebooks, maps, and a variety of other publications for hikers and the general public are also published. Membership application material, and a complete list of publications, with current prices, are available from the Conference by writing to the address below.

The Conference's headquarters is located at 799 Washington Street in Harpers Ferry, WV. Office hours are 9-5 weekdays and also on weekends from mid-May to the end of October. Write to:

APPALACHIAN TRAIL CONFERENCE
PO Box 807
Harpers Ferry, WV 25425-0807
Phone 304/535-6331
www.atconf.org

THE TRAIL IN PENNSYLVANIA

CHARACTER OF THE TRAIL ROUTE

From the Delaware Water Gap the Trail climbs over 1,100 feet, with view of the river below, before reaching Mt. Minsi. From here the Trail keeps generally to the ridge except for slight dips into Totts Gap and Fox Gap, and (after passing over Wolf's Rocks) a deeper dip into Wind Gap. The whole northern section of the Trail in Pennsylvania is lacking in springs that can be considered reliable after early summer.

After climbing out of Wind Gap, the Trail says on the ridge, crossing Smith Gap, dipping into and climbing out of Little Gap, and then passing over an open rocky area before dropping sharply into Lehigh Gap. Following the climb out of Lehigh Gap, the Trail stays on the ridge for nearly 30 miles before dropping down the side and passing near the Hawk Mountain Sanctuary at Eckville. A gradual climb then leads to the Pinnacle, the most spectacular viewpoint along the Trail in Pennsylvania.

The Trail next drops into Windsor Furnace before regaining the ridge, and then dropping steeply to the Schuykill River. Another 1,000-foot climb leads to 30 more miles of ridgetop hiking until the descent into Swatara Gap. Here the Trail leaves Blue Mountain and traverses St. Anthony's Wilderness, crossing Second Mountain, Sharp Mountain, Stony Mountain, and finally ascending Peters Mountain which it follows for about 15 miles before dropping steeply to the Susquehanna River.

Beyond the Susquehanna, the Trail turns toward the southwest, crossing Cove Mountain and Blue Mountain before entering the great Cumberland Valley. Here the Trail has been relocated to an off-road route thanks to land acquisitions by the National Park Service. At the southern edge of the valley the Trail climbs South Mountain and enters Michaux State Forest, passing through Pine Grove Furnace and Calendonia State Parks before leaving the plateau-like top of the south Mountain range and entering Maryland at Pen Mar.

HISTORY ALONG THE TRAIL

PRE-HISTORY AND HISTORY OF THE REGION

Topography. It is the arc of mountains extending from northeast to southwest in Pennsylvania that is essentially followed by the Appalachian Trail in its passage through the state. With some justification it has been argued that of all the natural features in the Keystone State none has influenced the course of history more than its mountains; and of those mountains, none carries more of history's mark than the ridges on which the A.T. finds itself. Not surprisingly therefore, the ebb and flow of historic events have left their traces in many places along the Trail's route. These signs are sometimes obvious, sometimes subtle and discernible only with some effort. Awareness of the impact of history on the region traversed by the A.T., however, can serve to enhance any hiking experience.

Native Americans. Often the first question that comes to the mind of a hiker in connection with speculation about the Native American use of the land through which the Trail happens to be passing concerns the identity of the particular tribe that inhabited the region. Such thinking, alas, goes instantly to the heart of much misunderstanding of the nature of Indian culture. Indians tended to move about considerably and the names by which they were known reflected their language or bloodlines rather than some particular area. Nevertheless, at the time of the arrival of the first European settlers, the Delaware River valley generally was occupied by the Lenni-Lenape, who spoke one of the Algonquian languages. It was the English settlers who assigned to them the name by which they are generally known: Delawares. By the late 1600s, however, this entire region was controlled by the Iroquois. Along with the Iroquois, the Delawares enjoyed a culture that had highly developed concepts of government, education, and morality. Although it lacked the intricate theological superstructure of the religions of the European settlers, the Delawares also had a finely developed religion.

The interaction between the Indian and European cultures is now known to have been much greater than is commonly realized. Indians provided the Europeans with their first introductions to such agricultural products as potatoes, corn, beans, squash, tomatoes, and tobacco. With less happy long-term results, they also introduced the new settlers to the joys of tobacco. The network of well-defined Indian paths (of which the Appalachian Trail, except for rare stretches, was not one) provided access to much of the interior of the province. The Indian languages also live on in a variety of ways, but mostly through a host of place names, not only in Pennsylvania but throughout most of the U.S.

The Europeans and the Indians. In general, the first Europeans to settle here were Scotch-Irish and German-speaking people, along with a few English, Welsh, and Dutch, most of who were fleeing the religious persecution and wars in Europe. Along with the settlers came missionaries of various persuasions seeking to convert the Indians. One of the most famous of the missionaries was Count Zinzendorff, under whose leadership a group of Moravians, settled Bethlehem in 1740. Another was Conrad Weiser, who grew up among the Mohawks and learned their language and customs. He became a trusted interpreter and intermediary between various Iroquois chiefs and the Penn family and other provincial officials.

West of the Susquehanna. By the late 1600s, the entire region west of the Susquehanna River was controlled by the Iroquois Indians, who in 1736 gave title to the region to the Penn family. Most of the early wagon trains heading for Ohio passed through Carlisle, not far from the present route of the A.T. In 1704, a licensed Indian trader, Jacques le Tort, was settled near Carlisle. Subsequently he gave his name to the famous trout stream in this area. Another early inhabitant was George Grogan, who settled in Crogans Gap (now Sterretts Gap) in 1741, about two miles from what is now the Appalachian Trail.

In Buchanan Valley, not far from the current site of Caledonia Park, is found another reminder of the Indian era in the South Mountain area. Near St. Ignatius Catholic Church is the statue of Mary Jemison, the "White Squaw," who as a girl of 15 was carried off by the Indians, taken first to Ohio, and later to the Genessee Valley near Letchworth Park in western New York. There she became an influential member of the tribe, twice marrying an Indian Chief, and living to the age of 90. In later life she declined an opportunity to return to the society of her childhood.

The Walking Purchase. One of the most interesting events to occur in the early 18th Century in this part of Pennsylvania was "The Walking Purchase," that took place in 1737. Settlers had for some time been pushing into this section, crowding the Indians from their lands. With tensions rising, a number of negotiations were held with the heirs of William Penn, as the result of which the Indians agreed to a novel method for determining territorial limits. The Penns would be granted land, the measurement of which was defined as what "a man walks in a day and a half." At that point, a line would be drawn straight to the Delaware River, and the boundaries would be defined. In the Indians' understanding of the arrangement, a day's walk meant the distance an Indian would normally cover in a day, allowing time to hunt, prepare meals, set up camp, and the like. In all probability, this would have been about 20 miles a day, or 30 miles in the stipulated day and a half.

Although there is no reason to believe that they did not fully understand the Indian concept of the agreement, the white men chose to interpret the definition as meaning the distance a man was *capable* of walking in a day and a half, rather than the distance normally covered. Moreover, instead of using only one man, they used three in relays, with the walking speed forced to nearly a run. The result was that from the starting point near Washington Crossing,

Pa. they managed to cover 61.25 miles. Then, instead of drawing the boundary line to hit the Delaware River at its nearest point, they contrived to come out near the Lackawaxen, thereby doubling the acreage the Indians had expected to grant them.

The Indians understandably accused the Penns of trickery and dishonesty, and among the Delaware Indians The Walking Purchase aroused bitter hatred for the whites. It was this smoldering resentment that a generation later was fanned into flames and erupted in the French and Indian War, causing great havoc throughout the region.

The French and Indian War. During the years of the French and Indian War (1754-1763) there were so many Indian attacks on settlements in this area that a line of forts and blockhouses was erected along the Blue Mountain ridge to protect the frontier. Extending from Easton to Mercersburg, this chain of structures generally paralleled the current route of the Appalachian Trail but was located lower down the mountain to be closer to the farms and settlements. An occasional lookout post was placed on top of the ridge.

The forts, generally at intervals of about 20 miles, were rather large stockades capable of holding a company of militia as well as several dozen families when the need arose. Between the forts, at about five-mile intervals, were smaller blockhouses, intended as only temporary shelter for a few families. Periodically the militia from the forts would check the blockhouses and escort any refugees to the larger fort. Although the chain was completed by 1756, it did not put an end to the Indian raids, but it was successful in giving the settlers some sense of security and a feeling that the government was doing something to protect them.

The government, however, was not protecting everyone equally. In December of 1763 a group of about 50 Scotch-Irish men, known as the Paxton Boys, set off from their base about a dozen miles south of where the Appalachian Trail now crosses the Susquehanna River to begin the bloody work that came to be known as the Conestoga Massacre. They rode to a tiny Lancaster County community inhabited by a small tribe of farming Indians, the

Conestogas. There the Paxton Boys killed and scalped a total of six women, old men, and a child. The 14 remaining inhabitants fled and pleaded for protection from the white officials of Lancaster, whereupon the Indians were locked in the jail for their own safety. Two weeks later, a larger group of about 100 Paxton Boys forced their way into the jail and hacked to death the remaining Conestogas. When they were finished, they had succeeded in killing in more or less horrible fashion a grand total of six old men, five women, six small boys, and three young girls. This trail of grisly cowardice prompted Benjamin Franklin to describe the Paxton Boys as "white savages."

Emboldened by their success, the Paxton Boys then set off for Philadelphia with the expressed intention of destroying a number of converted Indians who had fled from various Moravian settlements and eventually sought refuge in Philadelphia. This time, however, the Paxton Boys were intercepted at Germantown by a number of local citizens with fixed bayonets and artillery. In the face of cold steel and gun powder, the Paxton Boys were readily persuaded to return to their homes.

Even as enlightened citizens were deploring the depredations of the Paxton Boys, however, a bounty of $150 was being offered for each Delaware scalp. Understandably embittered by their treatment at the hands of the white settlers, most of the Delawares traveled west to Ohio and subsequently farther west and north. Today the scattered descendants of the Lenni-Lenape are to be found on reservations as far away as Oklahoma as well as at various locations in Canada. Indeed, throughout the French and Indian War, all of the Indian tribes were used as pawns in the global power struggle then under way between the English and the French.

EARLY INDUSTRY

Charcoal Iron. Of the early industries that have left a mark on the land still discernible to the passing Appalachian Trail hiker, three stand out: iron manufacturing, coal mining, and the railroads. Other commercial, though not strictly industrial enterprises from a somewhat later period that have also left traces are recreational/health resorts and an amusement park.

From 1740 until after the Civil War the charcoal iron industry flourished in Pennsylvania At its peak in about 1840 the charcoal iron industry employed more than 11,000 workers at 113 furnaces and 169 bloomeries, forges and rolling mills. (A bloomery, by the way, is a special hearth for smelting iron into shapes suitable for the production of wrought iron.) In many parts of southeastern and central Pennsylvania were found high quality iron ores much sought after by gun and tool makers. Nearby was generally an abundance of forest to provide the wood from which was produced the charcoal used to fuel the iron furnaces. The combination of these resources resulted in a thriving industry that lasted until the advent of coal as an iron-making fuel made the proximity of forests irrelevant.

Railroads. In the early 1800s, the railroad began to supplant the canals in Pennsylvania as the principal means of transporting goods and people. At the start of the Civil War, Pennsylvania had just under 2,600 miles of railroad track. By 1900, this mileage had grown to over 10,000. Although in recent years the railroads have dwindled dramatically and old lines by the hundreds have disappeared, the beds they followed are encountered everywhere in the back county. In many places, long stretches of former railroad bed have been turned into pleasant hiking paths. A number of these are encountered along the route of the A.T. in Pennsylvania.

Coal Mining. Although the route of the Appalachian Trail through Pennsylvania bypasses, happily, the major coal producing regions of the state, it does encounter in St. Anthony's Wilderness an area where some marginal coal seams were mined in the last century. The coal here was thin and quickly exhausted, leaving behind only some fascinating traces of a long-gone culture.

Health Resorts. In the 18th Century there sprang up at various locations in the Pennsylvania hills a number of resorts, catering to the affluent citizens of Philadelphia and other metropolitan centers. These resorts often offered mineral springs and other allegedly salubrious features to provide some extra justification for their existence, although one suspects that their clientele was chiefly motivated by nothing more than a desire to escape the unconditioned heat of urban summers in that era.

Amusement Resorts. Spawned by the railroad in its continuing effort to stimulate business, an amusement park was created near the Pennsylvania/Maryland border to which, in season, revelers were transported (by rail, of course) from more or less distant cities. With the spread of the motor car as a common mode of transportation, people were no longer so dependent on the railroad for their traveling, and the park closed down.

HISTORY OBSERVED FROM THE TRAIL

Franklin's Forts. Although the hiker will look in vain for any physical remains of Franklin's French and Indian War forts, there are markers here and there. Just west of PA Rt. 183, along the Appalachian Trail, is a historical marker for Fort Dietrich Snyder, which was supposedly a lookout post for Fort Northkill. Next came Fort Henry where there is another marker along the paved road. On the banks of the Susquehanna, a few miles south of where the Trail crosses, stood Fort Hunter, on whose foundations beside U.S. Rt. 22 a museum now stands.

Missionaries. Just off PA Rt. 501, near the A.T., is Pilger Ruh (Pilgrim's Rest) Spring, also called Ludwig's Brunnen. This was used by Conrad Weiser, interpreter and negotiator with the Indians, during his journey from Philadelphia to the Indian capitol of Shamokin (now Sunbury). The Moravian missionary Count Zinzendorff also used this route as early as 1742, as did Chief Shikellimy of the Iroquois Federation.

St. Anthony's Wilderness. Between Pa. Rt. 443 and Pa. Rt. 325, the Appalachian Trail passes through a magnificent stretch of wilderness unbroken by habitation for 14 miles. This land is now owned and managed by the Pennsylvania Game Commission. On a map that was probably printed just after the Revolution, and which is based on a 1770 map by W. Scull that was made for Thomas and Richard Penn, this area was designated as "St. Anthony's Wilderness."

Scattered through the area are a number of long abandoned coal mines which were in operation more than 100 years ago and were serviced by a branch of the Reading Railroad. The old rail bed, which now serves as a maintenance road for the Game Commission, follows Stony Creek for 15 miles from Gold Mine Road in the east to Ellendale Forge in the west. Stony Creek was the first stream in Pennsylvania designated as a "wild river" under the Commonwealth's Scenic Rivers Program.

The village of Rausch Gap, just off the A.T. near the maintenance road, flourished about 1850. Today little remains but a dry stone well about 20 feet from the Trail. The village at one time was populous enough to support a Catholic mission, and there is a small cemetery 150 feet away containing three gravestones of the John Proud family. The stones are dated 1853. If others were buried here, no stones remain to indicate it.

The Appalachian Trail follows an old stage coach road for many miles through the Wilderness. Side trails lead down to the sites of the railroad stations of Yellow Springs and Cold Springs. The last remains of the Cold Springs station were recently destroyed in the course of an effort to move it for restoration and salvage purposes.

For a number of years in the last Century the Jesuits of Philadelphia owned 60 acres at Cold Springs and maintained a summer school for six years. Then in 1880 they sold the property to a syndicate of Harrisburg men who built a summer hotel there at a time when mineral baths were very popular. As late as 1949 there was a YMCA camp at Cold Springs.

Iron Industry and Furnaces East of the Susquehanna.

At many places along the Appalachian Trail in Pennsylvania the hiker is likely to encounter flat round areas, between 30 and 50 feet in diameter. These are charcoal hearths where wood was burned to produce charcoal, which was used to fuel the iron furnaces that flourished from 1740 until after the Civil War.

Two miles down from the Trail on the Lehigh Furnace Gap Road are the ruins of the Lehigh Iron Furnace, built in 1826. The remains are 30 feet high and in fairly good condition.

Directly along the Trail, between Eckville and Port Clinton, is the site of the former Windsor Furnace. Nothing remains of this structure, although some glassy slag can still be found in the footpath. Iron stoves were a specialty, and its manufactures were said to include a replica in iron of The Last Supper.

The former Union Forge at Lickdale has also disappeared, but the ruins of the Manada Furnace can be found in the bushes along the Horse-Shoe Trail in Manada Gap, some nine miles south of the A.T. Elizabeth Furnace, once owned by "Baron" Stiegel, is on Pa. Rt. 501.

The last furnace near the Trail before reaching the Susquehanna River is Victoria Furnace, which was established around 1830, and remains in a good state of repair. It is located 1.5 miles down from the Trail on Clark's Creek, near Pa. Rt. 325, in back of Victoria Farms.

Pine Grove Furnace.

The basis of the iron and steel industry was the charcoal-fired blast furnace and forge of pre-Revolutionary times. In 1762 there was a furnace, owned by the Ege family, which is still standing at Boiling Springs, and one at Pine Grove, where firearms were made for the Revolution. By 1850 there were ten ironworks in the South Mountain area, most of which were on the Cumberland Valley side, but three were located near the present route of the A.T.

The Pine Grove Furnace was later acquired by the Watts family, who established a furnace, a forge, coal house, brick mansion house, smith and carpenter shops, 30 log dwellings, and grist and saw mills. The operation was supported by the charcoal that was produced from some 35,000 acres of land. Throughout this area are more of the charcoal hearths described above.

Most of the structures associated with the Pine Grove Furnace were destroyed by fire in 1915. All that survived were the mansion house, the furnace, and (a mile and a half away) Bunker Hill Farm (Rupp House), which later became the Potomac Appalachian Trail Club's Pine Grove Furnace Cabin. Greenish or bluish bits of the slag can still be found in the Trail in this area.

The railroad that serviced these works in the 1870s followed Mountain Creek up from Laurel Lake. This is the roadbed that is now used by the A.T. as it passes Fuller Lake, which was originally the 90-foot deep ore hole. Following a pump breakdown, the mine was flooded and later abandoned. Soon after 1893, the entire iron works operation closed down.

Caledonia Iron Works. The ruins of the Caledonia Iron Works furnace, which was built in 1837, can be seen in the parking lot at the corner of U.S. Rt. 30 and Pa. Rt. 233 in Caledonia State Park. The old blacksmith shop, which is right along the Trail, is now a museum. Thaddeus Stevens, the famous abolitionist, owned these works at the time of the Civil War. They were destroyed by Confederate troops en route to the Battle of Gettysburg in 1863.

Mt. Alto Iron Works. In the village of Mt. Alto, a few miles west of the Trail, iron works were in operation between 1807 and 1893. They consisted of a bloomery, which is a furnace for making wrought iron, as well as a refinery, shops, farms, and 20,000 acres of land. The Mt. Alto Iron Works employed 500 persons in its heyday. All that remains of the old forge on Little Antietam Creek is the name given to the Old Forge Picnic Grounds bordering the Trail.

Pen Mar Park. On the southern border of Pennsylvania, the Appalachian Trail runs through the old Pen Mar Park, which was built in 1878 and remained for more than 60 years one of the most famous resorts in the East. The park was owned by the Western Maryland Railway, which ran many excursion trains there, bringing clubs, Sunday School picnic groups, and similar organizations for a summer outing. A feature of the park was an observatory platform at High Rock, from which Chambersburg could be seen 24 miles in the distance. The park also included a fun house, a roller coaster, a miniature railroad, resort hotels, and restaurants. It is said that the average attendance for such picnics was 7,000 people, with the record having been set by a Lutheran gathering that numbered 15,000.

Half way up to High Rock the railroad built the Blue Mountain House Hotel in 1883. This was a great rambling frame building that could accommodate 400 guests. It was destroyed in 1913 in a fire that could be seen from Waynesboro, Pa., many miles away. Another large hotel along the Trail in southern Pennsylvania was the Buena Vista Springs Hotel, where it was said there were more servants than guests. It is now a Catholic seminary.

With the coming of the automobile and a restless generation searching for new adventures, the railroad found that Pen Mar Park was no longer profitable. It was leased to another company for a time, and continued operation until 1943 when, as the result of World War II gas rationing, it was closed and the buildings were removed.

The editor is particularly indebted to Bruce Bomberger of the Pennsylvania Historical and Museum Commission for his invaluable advice and guidance in connection with the preparation of this section.

Acknowledgment is also made of extensive reliance on "A History of Pennsylvania" by Philip S. Klein and Ari Hoogenboom; Published by McGraw-Hill, Inc.; 1973.

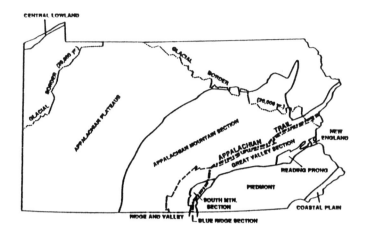

GEOLOGY ALONG THE TRAIL

Introduction. The Appalachian Trail passes through three sections of two physiographic provinces in its 230-mile traverse across the state from the Delaware Water Gap to Pen Mar. These three physiographic regions are:

1. Appalachian Mountain section of the Ridge and Valley province;
2. Great Valley section of the Ridge and Valley province; and
3. South Mountain section of the Blue Ridge province.

Each one of these areas, shown on the accompanying map, has a characteristic topography that reflects the various rock types present and the geologic history of those rocks. The three sections are described as follows:

APPALACHIAN MOUNTAIN SECTION:
Ridge and Valley Province

This division extends from the Delaware Water Gap 160.6 miles to Pa. 944 west of the Susquehanna River, and includes Trail Sections 1 through 9. The topography is characterized by long, narrow ridges separated by narrow valleys. The ridges are steep-sided, linear mountains with undulating crest lines that are broken periodically by wind gaps and water gaps. These crests are underlain by erosion-resistant quartzites and conglomerates that frequently crop out and are the source of the rock debris often present on the ridge slopes. The ridges sometimes turn back on themselves after long uninterrupted straight stretches in a pattern that reveals the nature of deformed bedrock masses folded into broad anticlines (upfolds) and synclines (downfolds). The mountains rise about 1,000 feet above adjacent valleys which are underlain by more easily eroded shale, siltstone, and limestone.

Bedrock in these mountains ranges in age from 440 to 320 million years; it is sandstone, quartzite, siltstone, conglomerate, shale, and a little coal. Rocks beyond the horizon to the north are younger and those in the valley to the south are older. All of these rock units were deformed by mountain building activity which culminated about 270 million years ago, and changed the original horizontal attitude of the rocks into that of steeply dipping, near vertical, or overturned beds. Millions of years of subsequent erosion has produced the landscape present today.

About 20,000 years ago a continental glacier of thick, scouring ice extended south into Pennsylvania intercepting the area of the Trail in a small section near Delaware Water Gap (see map). Two older continental glaciations, one about 150,000 years ago and the other more than 700,000 years ago occupied the valleys on either side of the ridge in Trail Sections 1, 2, and 3. There is no evidence, however, that either glaciation covered the ridge. During these glacial periods, climatic conditions in Pennsylvania beyond the ice border were severe and most non-glaciated areas probably had permafrost to some depth. Repetitive freeze-thaw cycles occurred everywhere, particularly on south-facing slopes at higher elevations. These cycles subjected the ridge-crest rocks to ice wedging in open, water-saturated fractures. Rock fragments broke away from ridge-crest outcrops and slid down the slopes where they

23

accumulated as large masses of talus (or scree). Some gaps in the mountain crest are floored with boulder fields derived from this debris. Broken, angular rock fragments and broken outcrops common along the ridge crest are a product of this climate-induced, physical disintegration of rock.

GREAT VALLEY SECTION:
Ridge and Valley Province

This division extends from Pa. Rt. 944 at the foot of Blue Mountain 13.8 miles to Yellow Breeches Creek at the foot of South Mountain. It includes Trails Section 10 and part of 11. The topography is characterized by a broad, open undulating valley, part of the Great Valley section extending from central New York through Virginia into Tennessee. The Trail crosses this valley at one of its narrow points (approximately 12 miles) in order to reach South Mountain which merges into the massive Blue Ridge Mountain farther south.

This valley is underlain by intensely deformed limestone, dolomite and shale with narrow, cross-cutting diabase dikes. The limestone, dolomite, and shale range in age from 560 to 440 million years, while the diabase is approximately 180 million years old. All the rock units except the diabase weather readily in the humid Northeast climate. The diabase is more resistant to erosion than the adjacent rocks, standing as a narrow ridge across part of the valley. The Trail follows part of this "Iron-Stone Ridge."

SOUTH MOUNTAIN SECTION:
Blue Ridge Province

This division extends from the Yellow Breeches 56 miles to Pen Mar and beyond, including part of Trail Section 11 and all of Sections 12 through 14. The topography is characterized by rounded, relatively gentle knobs ranging in elevation from about 550 to 1,190 feet above the valley floor. White Rocks, near the northeastern tip of the province, is an exception; there the topography is steep and rugged, and capped by a spine of hard, vitreous quartzite bedrock.

The rocks of South Mountain are the oldest encountered along the Trail in Pennsylvania, ranging in age from about 600 to 560 million years. These rocks also exhibit the most complex geologic relationships. The mountain range is a broad, composite, anticlinal (upfold) structure that has been thrust and overturned along deep-seated, regional fault zones during crustal shortening. Bedrock is composed of vitreous quartzite, phyllite, conglomeratic quartzite, graywacke and metamorphosed volcanic rocks, all of which are more resistant to erosion than rocks in adjoining valleys.

The geology of the Appalachian Trail in Pennsylvania is described in greater detail in a publication by the Pennsylvania Geological Survey done in cooperation with Keystone Trails Association. It is entitled *The Geology of the Appalachian Trail in Pennsylvania,* (General Geology Report 74), and contains a full-color geologic map inside the back cover. The book is available from the Pennsylvania Department of General Services, State Book Store, 1825 Stanley Drive, Harrisburg, Pa. 17103; telephone 717/787-5109.

NOTE: The foregoing section on "Geology" was originally prepared for the eighth edition of this Guide by John P. (Pete) Wilshusen, a longtime KTA member and a retired member of the staff of the Pennsylvania Topographic and Geologic Survey. Pete died shortly after the publication of the eighth edition, and this section was reviewed and slightly revised by W. D. Sevon, also of the Pennsylvania Geologic Survey.

HAWK MOUNTAIN SANCTUARY

The Appalachian Trail passes through a corridor adjacent to the eastern boundary of one of the most famous wildlife areas in the world-Hawk Mountain Sanctuary. The Sanctuary is accessible to A.T. hikers by a blue-blazed side trail which continues along the ridge after the A.T. drops down through the valley to the south or heads north towards PA Rt. 309.

The Sanctuary, founded in 1934, was the first refuge developed to protect birds of prey as they migrated along the ridge in the fall of the year. Prior to its establishment, Hawk Mountain was the gathering place for hundreds of gunners who would engage in the wholesale slaughter of hawks, falcons, and eagles as the birds passed by the North Lookout.

Now persons come from around the world to visit the Sanctuary throughout the year. The greatest influx of visitors comes in the autumn to view the spectacle of the migration. From mid-August through mid-December some 30,000 birds of prey of 14 species can be seen, sometimes at remarkable close range, from one of several lookout points accessible by footpaths.

Early September brings the American Bald Eagle followed by the great Broad-Winged Hawk migration in mid-September. Broad Wings can be seen in "kettles" of a hundred or more spirating above the outlooks. October is best for the largest variety of hawks as wells as the southward movements of water fowl. It is also the peak of the autumn coloration. Visitors in late November stand a chance, especially on strong northwest winds, of seeing the Golden Eagle.

The Visitor Center includes exhibits featuring bird of prey ecology and migration, a bookshop, and windows overlooking a feeding station. During all there are illustrated lectures on Saturday evenings in the Amphitheater.

Since the Sanctuary is a private, non-profit educational institution an admission fee is collected. Hikers are encouraged to use the honor system by making an effort to cover the $4.00 ($6.00 between mid August to December) admission charge when they arrive, either by stopping at the

Visitor Center entrance gate in the fall, or speaking to a staff member on the North Lookout.

Membership in the Hawk Mountain Sanctuary Association allows free admission to the trails as well as many other benefits. No camping, fires, or pets are allowed on Sanctuary property or along the clearly marked Hawk Mountain/A.T. Corridor.

For further information write:

Hawk Mountain Sanctuary
Route #2
Kempton, PA 19529
www.hawkmountain.org

LAND OWNERSHIP

PENNSYLVANIA GAME COMMISSION

The Pennsylvania Game Commission established in 1895, owns nearly 1.4 million acres of land in Pennsylvania. The land is managed for the propagation and preservation of wildlife. The agency is self-supporting and receives the major portion of its income from hunting and trapping license sales, timber sales, and federal aid reimbursements. The Commission is an independent administrative state agency providing Commonwealth citizens with the opportunity both to hunt and to enjoy wildlife on a nonconsumptive basis. The Game Commission recognizes the use of State Game Lands by non-hunters such as photographers, birders, and hikers, and encourages these activities. Financial support of the Game Commission by non-hunters is welcome. Such support can be through the purchase of a license or by participating in programs designed to benefit nongame wildlife. Funds for these programs are raised through sales of wildlife stamps, patches, and prints. Direct contributions can also be made to specific nongame programs such as "Working Together for Wildlife."

The Game Commission has extensive holdings on Blue Mountain, which is the basic route of the Appalachian Trail from west of the Susquehanna River to the Delaware Water Gap. As a result, 72 miles of Appalachian Trail in this section traverses through and is protected by the State Game Lands.

Camping and establishing campsites are prohibited on State Game Lands. The only exceptions are a few designated areas such as the Rausch Gap Shelter in Game Lands #211. Here, because there is extensive mileage in both directions on the Appalachian Trail within the boundaries of the Game Lands, this shelter was authorized for the use of through-hikers passing through St. Anthony's Wilderness. Hikers may stay at the shelter for only one night. The Game Commission does permit primitive camping along the Appalachian Trail as it traverses Game Lands.

The rules for primitive camping by A.T. through-hikers in State Game Lands are as follows:

1. Camp within 200 feet of the Trail
2. Camp one night only at any given site.
3. Do **NOT** camp within 500 feet of a water source or public access.
4. **NO** open fires during times of fire hazard.

For more information about Pennsylvania State Game Lands, write:

Pennsylvania Game Commission
2001 Elmerton Avenue
Harrisburg, PA 17110-9797
717-787-4250
http://www.pgc.state.pa.us

PENNSYLVANIA BUREAU OF FORESTRY

Forty-five miles of the Appalachian Trail in Pennsylvania are located on State Forest lands. About 39 miles are on the Michaux State Forest, which the A.T. crosses shortly after it enters the state from the south. The remaining six miles are divided between the Weiser and Delaware State Forests.

The purpose of the State Forests, according to law, is: "To provide a continuous supply of timber, lumber, wood and other forest products, to protect the watersheds, conserve the waters, and regulate the flow of rivers and streams of the state, and to furnish opportunities for healthful recreation to the public." State Forest lands are open for the enjoyment of the public by their administrators, the Bureau of Forestry of the Department of Conservation and Natural Resources.

The most valuable resource on the Michaux State forest is water. All or part of fifteen municipal watersheds are located on the Michaux State Forest, and collectively they comprise approximately 24% of the total acreage in this forest district. As you walk the Appalachian Trail you will be in or very close to many of these watersheds.

On State Forest lands the Appalachian Trail is contained within a buffer zone where timber harvesting is restricted to the removal of hazardous trees that pose a risk to public safety. Outside the buffer zone, various types of cutting practices are used by the Bureau of Forestry to provide a continuous supply of wood products and to enhance the quality of various wildlife habitats. The hiker who ventures off the main trail may have the opportunity to see various stages of forest progression and encounter a wider diversity of both plants and animals. These side trails generally lead to local points of interest, springs, camping areas, rock outcroppings or scenic overlooks.

Camping is permitted along the main Trail and along most of the side trails on State Forest land. Small cooking and warming fires are permitted where adequate precautions are taken to prevent the spread of fire into the forest. All fires are prohibited when the forest fire danger is <u>high</u>, <u>very high</u>, or <u>extreme</u>.

For information about State forest land, contact:

Pennsylvania Department of Conservation and Natural Resources
Bureau of Forestry
PO Box 8552
Harrisburg, PA 17105
717-783-7941
E-mail: ask.dcnr@a1.dcnr.state.pa.us
http://www.dcnr.state.pa.us

PENNSYLVANIA BUREAU OF STATE PARKS

<u>Caledonia State Park</u>, 40 Rocky Mountain Road, Fayetteville, PA 17222-9610 (717/352-2161; caledonia.sp@a1.dcnr.state.pa.us; fax 717/352-7026) is one of the oldest State Parks in Pennsylvania. Located in Franklin and Adams Counties midway between Chambersburg and Gettysburg, it is on U.S. Route 30.

Pine Grove Furnace State Park, 1100 Pine Grove Road, Gardners, PA 17324-8837 (717/486-7174; fax 717/486-4961; pinegrove.sp@a1.dcnr.state.pa.us) is located in the heart of Michaux State Forest in southern Cumberland County. The park took its name from the Pine Grove Iron Furnace, the remains of which still stand. The furnace dates back to 1764. Other buildings dating back to the old iron making community also still remain. The historic significance of the area was recognized in 1977 when the iron making area was entered in the National Register of Historical Places.

The first recreational facilities were built in the area by the railroad. The area was later purchased by the Commonwealth of Pennsylvania in 1913.

Two small lakes are situated within the 696-acre mountain park. The first–Fuller Lake, 1.7 acres in size–was the ore hole from which the iron ore was mined for Pine Grove Furnace. The Fuller Lake recreation area includes facilities for swimming, picnicking, family camping, organized youth group tenting, and fishing.

The second lake is the 25-acre Laurel Lake, where picnicking, swimming, nonpower boating, and fishing facilities are available. The Appalachian Trail passes through the central portion of the park. A parking area near the old iron furnace is provided for the parking of trail hikers' vehicles. Register the vehicle at the park office. A hiker's log is also kept at the camp store, which is open during the summer season.

Located along the Appalachian Trail, as hikers enter the park from the south, the Ironmaster's Mansion is now an AYH Hostel. Overnight lodging, hot showers, cooking facilities, a game room, and a hot tub are available for hikers. Contact the hostel at 717/486-7575 for more information.

Swatara State Park, c/o Memorial Lake State Park, R.R. 1, Box 7045, Grantville, PA 17028-9682 (717/865-6470; memorial.sp@a1.dcnr.state.pa.us; fax 717/865-7289) consists of 3,516 acres extending northeast from Swatara Gap for 7.5 miles along the Swatara Creek Valley. Currently undeveloped, the park nevertheless offers recreational opportunities for hiking, hunting, bicycling, fishing, canoeing and rafting, and ski touring.

Provisions are being made to provide a protected corridor for the Appalachian Trail, which passes through the southwestern portion of the park.

For general information about Pennsylvania's State Parks, contact:

Pennsylvania Department of Conservation and Natural
Resources
Bureau of State Parks
P.O. Box 8551
Harrisburg, Pennsylvania 17105-8551
1-800-63 PARKS
http://www.dcnr.state.pa.us

PENNSYLVANIA FISH AND BOAT COMMISSION

At Boiling Springs the Trail follows a route along the shore of Children's Lake, using a corridor that was acquired by the Trust for Appalachian Trail Lands with the help of a local benefactor and the Pennsylvania Fish And Boat Commission. Management of the lake is the responsibility of the Fish And Boat Commission.

NATIONAL PARK SERVICE

Pursuant to passage in 1968 of the National Trails System Act, which established the Appalachian Trail as one of the nation's first two National Scenic Trails, the National Park Service (NPS) has undertaken to protect those miles of the Trail that are outside existing state and federal units, and which could not be covered by state protection programs.

NPS's protection program in Pennsylvania is now about 96% complete. Eventually nearly 100 miles of the Trail in Pennsylvania will lie in a protected corridor on lands acquired by NPS. In addition to making the necessary connections between existing public lands, the Trail corridor was located to favor the highest land, minimize impacts to private landowners, and take advantage of features attractive to hikers.

In an unprecedented move, the National Park Service in 1984 conveyed to ATC management responsibility for recently acquired NPS lands outside existing federally administered areas. ATC, in turn, has assigned responsibility to its appropriate member clubs. The National Park Service retains a responsibility and an interest in seeing that these lands and their resources are managed "to provide for maximum outdoor recreation potential and for the conservation and enjoyment of the nationally significant scenic, historic, natural or cultural qualities of the areas through which such trails may pass." (Sec. 3b of the National Trails System Act)

The National Park Service remains an active and committed partner in the cooperative management of the Appalachian Trail.

PRIVATE LAND

Although a very high percentage of the Trail in Pennsylvania is now on publicly owned land, there remain a number of sections that continue to make use of private property. The owners of this property have every right to expect that their lands will be treated with respect. Failure to do so can lead to needless controversy and difficult problems for trail managers. As noted above, the hiker should leave no trace of passage. In particular, please note the following:

- Do not destroy or damage trees.
- Do not damage fences or leave gates open.
- Do not litter the trail.
- Do not disturb crops or animals.
- Be careful of fires; build them only at designated camp sites.
- Carry out your trash. (If you carried it in, you can carry it out.)
- Take nothing but pictures; leave nothing but footprints.

GENERAL INFORMATION

TRAIL MAINTENANCE

The work of maintaining the shelters and cabins, and keeping the trails cleared and blazed is done by volunteers-approximately 15,000 hours per year. No one is paid for any trail work. Each section of the Trail is assigned to a club. You will find the name of the maintaining organization or organizations at the beginning of each Trail Description Section under General Information.

Although you are certainly encouraged to toss aside blowdowns and to clean up around shelters, you should not attempt to do any trail marking or relocating on your own. Instead, join a hiking club and offer your services through it. For a list of the names and addresses of organizations affiliated with Keystone Trails Association, write to KTA, Box 251, Cogan Station, PA 17728. Any unusual trouble spots along the Trail should be reported to KTA at the above address or to the Appalachian Trail Conference, Box 807, Harpers Ferry, WV 25425.

RIDGERUNNER PROGRAM

While hiking the Trail you may meet a Ridgerunner, an individual hired through the Appalachian Trail Conference, to hike sections of the Trail. The primary goal of the Ridgerunner is to provide information and education to users of the backcountry by explaining existing rules, regulations, and low impact practices, to monitor the trail and assist local trail managers. Through the Ridgerunner program the Trail and the environment are protected and hikers benefit from important information or assistance.

The Ridgerunner Program is financially supported by the PA Department of Conservation and Natural Resources, Appalachian Trail Conference, Wilmington Trail Club, Batona Hiking Club, AMC-Delaware Valley Chapter, Philadelphia Trail Club, Mountain Club of Maryland, Susquehanna A.T. Club, Cumberland Valley Appalachian Trail Management Association, and the Potomac Appalachian Trail Club.

MAINTAINING CLUBS IN PENNSYLVANIA

The Appalachian Trail in Pennsylvania is maintained by the following volunteer clubs, listed from north to south:

Wilmington Trail Club	Delaware River to Fox Gap
Batona Hiking Club	Fox Gap to Wind Gap
Appalachian Mountain Club Delaware Valley Chapter	Wind Gap to Little Gap
Philadelphia Trail Club	Little Gap to Lehigh Furnace Gap
Blue Mountain Eagle Climbing Club	Lehigh Furnace Gap to Bake Oven Knob Road
	Tri-County Corner to Rausch Gap
Allentown Hiking Club	Bake Oven Knob Road to Tri-County Corner
Brandywine Valley Outing Club	Rausch Gap to Pa. Route 325
Susquehanna Appalachian Trail Club	Pa. Route 325 to Pa. Route 225
York Hiking Club	Pa. Route 225 to Susquehanna River
Mountain Club of Maryland	Susquehanna River to Darlington Trail
	Center Point Knob to Pine Grove Furnace
Cumberland Valley Appalachian Trail Management Association	Darlington Trail to Center Point Knob
Potomac Appalachian Trail Club- North Chapter	Pine Grove Furnace to Pen Mar

The accompanying diagram, "Pennsylvania Appalachian Trail Maintenance Assignments" depicts the relative maintenance responsibility of each club.

MAILING ADDRESSES

Shown below are the mailing addresses of each of the Pennsylvania maintaining clubs. It should be noted, however, that in the case of some of the clubs, the mailing address tends to change with each change of club leadership. If you are unable to reach a club at the address given, write to Keystone Trails Association, Box 251, Cogan Station, PA 17728-0251, for a copy of the latest KTA Directory, which will give you the current address for each of the clubs, as well as much of the information about KTA.

Allentown Hiking Club

P.O. Box 1542
Allentown, PA
18105-1542

Appalachian Mountain Club
Delaware Valley Chapter

c/o William Steinmetz
1180 Greenleaf Dr.
Bethlehem, PA
18017-9319

Batona Hiking Club

c/o Bette Irwin, 150 North
Bethlehem Pike, D-10
Ambler, PA 19002

Blue Mountain Eagle
Climbing Club

P.O. Box 14982
Reading, PA 19612-4982

Brandywine Valley Outing Club

Box 134
Rockland, DE 19732

Cumberland Valley A.T.
Management Association

P.O. Box 395
Boiling Springs, PA
17007-0395

Mountain Club of Maryland

c/o Paul Ives
802 Kingston Road
Baltimore, MD 21212

Philadelphia Trail Club

Edward Kenna
741 Golf Drive
Warrington, PA 18976

Potomac Appalachian Trail Club
- North Chapter

118 Park Street, SW,
Vienna, VA 22180

Susquehanna Appalachian
Trail Club

P.O. Box 61001
Harrisburg, PA
17106-1001

York Hiking Club

c/o John Seville
2684 Forest Rd
York, PA 17402

Wilmington Trail Club

P.O Box 1184
Wilmington, DE 19899

PENNSYLVANIA APPALACHIAN TRAIL
MAINTENANCE ASSIGNMENTS

Maintaining Organization	Club Mileage	Miles*	Boundary Feature
		0.0	Delaware Water Gap
Wilmington Trail Club	7.2		
		7.2	Fox Gap
Batona Hiking Club	8.6		
		15.8	Wind Gap
AMC - Del Valley Chapter	15.4		
		31.2	Little Gap
Philadelphia Trail Club	10.3		
		41.5	Lehigh Furnace Gap
BMECC	3.4		
		44.9	Bake Oven Knob Road
Allentown Hiking Club	10.3		
		55.3	Tri-County Corner
Blue Mountain Eagle Climbing Club (BMECC)	61.8		
		117	Rausch Gap
Brandywine Valley Outing Club	11		
		128	PA Rt 325
Susquehanna A.T. Club	9.4		
		137.4	PA Rt 225
York Hiking Club	7.2		
		144.6	Susquehanna River
Mountain Club of Maryland	12.7		
		157.3	Darlington Trail
Cumberland Valley A.T. Management Association	17.2		
		174.5	Center Point Knob
Mountain Club of Maryland	16.7		
		191.2	Pine Grove Furnace
Potomac Appalachian Trail Club - North Chapter	37.6		
		228.8	Pen Mar

* Miles are cumulative from N to S

38

MEASUREMENTS

Distances in this guide book are given in traditional units; e.g., miles, yards, feet. For the benefit of those readers who may be interested, a metric conversion table is printed near the front of this book.

TRAIL MARKINGS

On some highways the point where the Appalachian Trail crosses is marked by a large brown wood signboard, of which about 100 have been erected by the Pennsylvania Department of Transportation as a public service.

The Trail itself through woods and along roads is marked by white retangular paint blazes on trees, p;ower or telephone poles, and occasionally on rocks. The standard size for paint blazes is two inches wide by six inches long. Blazes are applied in a vertical position. Also, at intervals the Trail is marked by diamond-shaped metal markers, reading **"APPLACHIAN TRAIL - MAINE TO GEORGIA"**. The paint blazes are at frequent intervals, and hikers should have no difficulty following the Trail if they watch for the blazes.

A "double blaze" (two blazes, one above the other with a space between) is placed as a warning sign. If may indicate an obscure turn or change in direction which might not otherwise be noticed; or if may indicate a change in trail conditions, such as difficult footing.

A hiker should not go more than a quarter of a mile without seeing a blaze or other Trail indication. If this happens, retrace your steps until you again encounter blazes. Then proceed with caution. Recent timbering operations may have created complications. In such areas use extreme caution. Trail relocations are normally indicated by signs. Blue blazes indicate a side trail to a spring, viewpoint shelter, or an access trail.

Yellow blazes are used by State Parks for their boundaries. The yellow blazes of the Horse-Shoe Trail are seen only at its junction with the Appalachian Trail north of Harrisburg. Blue blazes are used for the Tuscarora Trail. Other colors are used on other trails. State Forest and State Game Land boundaries are marked with non-uniform white blazes where can be confusing to hikers. Use caution.

SHELTERS AND CABINS

Open three or four-sided shelters are located along the Trail at varying distances. A spring or other water source is usually nearby.

The shelters were constructed for the benefit of hikers not for picnickers. All hikers may use them on a "first-come first-served" basis and for one night only. They should be shared to the limit of their capacity. Be hospitable, courteous, clean, and neat. Leave a clean camp with firewood for the next comer. Burn or take home all refuse and tin cans. If you carry it in, you carry it out even when in a fireplace.

A number of shelters have composting privies. These privies are installed and maintained by volunteers at a considerable expense. For these privies to work effectively garbage and trash must not be placed into the privy and liquid waste should be minimized. For everyone's enjoyment please cooperate.

Unfortunately certain shelters have proven to be highly attractive to vandals. The damage done by these inconsiderate persons and the condition which vandalized shelters are sometimes left can render them virtually uninhabitable. Trail maintainers have had to expend an inordinate amount of time, energy, and money simply to keep some shelters usable. In some cases shelters have been so extensively damaged that they had to be substantially rebuilt. In some extreme cases shelters have been dismantled and removed. The difficult tasks often encountered in maintaining a shelter have caused problems even in recruiting volunteers willing to accept such an assignment.

All shelter users are encouraged to do whatever they can to encourage respect for these structures and to help reduce the level of vandalism and abuse.

In the division south of the Susquehanna River are four locked cabins managed by the Potomac Appalachian Trail Club. To use these cabins, reservations must be made in advance at PATC's Headquarters, 118 Park St., S.W., Vienna, VA 22180. Keys will be supplied for definite dates and a fee is charged for the use of these cabins.

MAPS

A series of maps showing the route of the Appalachian Trail and connecting side trails throughout Pennsylvania is published by Keystone Trails Association. The maps are specifically designed for use with this guidebook. They can be obtained from KTA (PO Box 251, Cogan Station, PA 17728-0251) or from the Appalachian Trail Conference. Write for a current price list.

For the portion of the Pennsylvania A.T. between the Susquehanna River and Pen Mar maps are also published by the Potomac Appalachian Trail Club (PATC). These can be used in connection with this guidebook if you prefer. They can be ordered from PATC, 118 Park Street, S.W. Vienna, VA 22180

For those desiring more detailed topographic information, the USGS 7 1/2' quadrangle maps are available. They can be purchased from the U.S. Geological Survey, Box 25286, Denver Federal Center, Building 810, Denver, CO 80225. The appropriate quadrangles for the Appalachian Trail are listed below. It is important to note that the A.T. may or may not be shown on these maps, and that when shown, may not be accurate because of the relocations that have occurred over the years. It is suggested that if these maps are to be used, the actual route should be transferred to them from current KTA maps.

Detailed maps and other publications about the geology of the Trail in Pennsylvania are shown in a free "List of Publications," which is available from: DEP, Geologic Survey, PO Box 2357, Harrisburg, Pa. 17120.

PA. A.T. SECTIONS	USGS QUADRANGLES
Delaware Water Gap to Lehigh Gap	Stroudsburg Saylorsburg Wind Gap Kunkletown Palmerton

Lehigh Gap to Schuylkill Gap	Palmerton Lehighton Slatedale New Tripoli New Ringgold Hamburg Auburn
Schuylkill Gap to Swatara Gap	Auburn Friedensburg Swatara Hill Pine Grove Fredericksburg Indiantown Gap
Swatara Gap to Susquehanna River	Indiantown Gap Tower City Grantville Enders Halifax Duncannon
Susquehanna River to Pa. Rt. 94	Duncannon Wertzville Mechanicsburg Dillsburg Mt. Holly Springs
Pa. Rt. 94 to Caledonia	Mt. Holly Springs Dickinson Walnut Bottom Caledonia Park
Caledonia to Pen Mar	Caledonia Park Iron Springs Waynesboro Blue Ridge Summit Smithburg

SUGGESTIONS FOR HIKERS

SAFETY AND SECURITY

Although criminal acts are probably less common on the Appalachian Trail than in most other human environments, they do occur. Crimes of violence, up to and including murder and rape, have taken place at various times over the years. It should be noted, however, that such serious crimes on the A.T. have a frequency rate on the order of perhaps one per year or less. Even if such events are less common on the Trail than elsewhere, they can be more difficult to deal with because of the remoteness of most of the Trail, even in a state as relatively developed as Pennsylvania. When hiking you must assume the need for at least the same level of prudence as you would exercise if walking the streets of a strange city or an unknown neighborhood.

A few elementary suggestions can be noted. Above all, it is best not to hike alone. Be cautious of strangers. Be sure that family and/or friends know your planned itinerary and timetable. If you customarily use a "trail name," your home contacts should know what it is. Although telephones are rarely handy along the Trail unless you have a cellular telephone, if you can reach one, the "911" emergency line is now in use throughout most of Pennsylvania. Many sections of the A.T. in the Commonwealth are actually on county lines. Since 911 accesses you to the county control, it is important that you know your location so that the closest emergency response unit is alerted.

The carrying of firearms is <u>not</u> recommended. The risks of accidental injury or death far outweigh any self-defense value that might result from arming oneself. In any case, guns are illegal on National Park Service lands and in certain other jurisdictions as well.

The Appalachian Trail Conference, with the cooperation of Trail groups in Pennsylvania and elsewhere, has embarked on a program of developing an emergency information network. When complete, it will result in the posting of emergency information at shelters and other key points along the Trail. Pertinent information will be included in future editions of this and other guidebooks, and will be publicized in other ways as well. In the meantime, be prudent and cautious without allowing common sense to slip into paranoia.

FIRES

The use of small stoves for cooking is recommended in preference to building wood fires, both for safety reasons and to minimize the growing demand for dead wood for such fires. If you do use wood fires, use low impact camping methods. Use existing fire rings at established campsites. Building a mound fire or using a portable fire pan are two types of low impact campfires that will minimize scaring of the land. A mound fire is built by placing several inches of soil on a fire proof material laid on the ground. The fire is built on top of the soil. The fire pan is used in a similar way. After the fire is out the ashes are spread and the soil is returned to original location. Remember that smaller fires are more efficient than large ones. Avoid putting Styrofoam, aluminum, and plastic in the campfire as this is not recommended for the environment.

Fires are permitted in State Forests at shelters, fireplaces or picnic grounds, except during periods of high fire danger. Fires should be completely extinguished by pouring water on them. At shelters, leave a supply of wood in a sheltered place for the next arrivals.

In State Game Lands, camping is not permitted except at officially authorized sites or as otherwise authorized by Game Commission regulations. (See the section on the Pennsylvania Game Commission earlier in this Guide.)

WATER

While hiking the A.T. in Pennsylvania, you will encounter water sources such as springs, brooks, and streams at frequent intervals along the Trail. Because the route follows ridge tops for much of its length, however, many water sources tend to dry up during the summer.

> All such water sources found along the Trail should be assumed to be **CONTAMINATED.**

The mentioning of these sources in this Guide and on the accompanying maps in no way implies their suitability for use. KTA, ATC and all member clubs and agents expressly disclaim liability for any impurities in such water.

It is best to carry water known to be safe, and to be prepared to use some purification method when using any water source whose purity is in doubt. Take particular care that you do not cause the contamination of water sources. Never wash dishes, clothes or hands in the water source. Make sure food and human wastes are buried well away from any water source.

It is perhaps useful to mention Giardiasis, an intestinal disorder that occurs with some frequency. It is caused by a microorganism that can be found in untreated "natural" water. The organism, Giardia, is killed at temperatures below boiling. Consequently, boiling water for one minute ensures that the water has been raised to a sufficient temperature to destroy them. This is the preferred treatment. Water filters are also available to aid in the removal of Giardia. Giardiasis can be temporarily incapacitating, but is not ordinarily life threatening.

SNAKES

Snakes may be encountered while hiking the A.T. in Pennsylvania. Contrary to some popular stories, snakes are shy and retiring, and avoid confrontations with humans whenever possible. Two poisonous varieties may be found here: copperheads and timber rattlesnakes. Both species unfortunately are becoming increasingly rare. If you are careful and quiet, you may be lucky enough to sight one of these inhabitants of Penn's Woods.

The danger from them is small if reasonable care is taken while on the trail. Do not blindly put your hands or feet into openings in rock crevices or ledges. Look carefully before you step into a hidden spot, such as the other side of a log. Move through underbrush with caution.

Given notice, both copperheads and rattlesnakes will move out of your way. If you wish to avoid them, you can usually do so by letting them know you are coming. One overseer of an A.T. section in Pennsylvania gave the following directions for traversing a rock field on his section of trail where a family of copperheads was known to make its home. Obtain a stick or use your walking stick, if you have one. Tap one the rocks ahead of you as you traverse the rock field. The sounds will set the copperheads scurrying to safety.

In case you are bitten, the safest course is to stop, wait, and send for help. In Pennsylvania help is not too distant from the A.T. Amateur use of snake bit kits can be dangerous and is of dubious value. While very painful, snake bites are rarely fatal, particularly if professional treatment is obtained in a reasonable amount of time.

DOGS

While they may make fine companions for trail hikers, dogs present several problems. When running loose, they often frighten other hikers and wildlife. When the Trail crosses or comes near private land, dogs may trespass on private property to the annoyance of the owner. It is strongly recommended that dogs be under control at all times when other hikers are nearby and when the trail is on or near private land. In this way your own happy sojourn in the woods will not be at the expense of another hiker's enjoyment, nor will it generate ill will toward the A.T.

RABIES

In recent years the incidence of rabies in Pennsylvania has been increasing, largely in wild animals. Hikers should accordingly be aware of the existence of the problem and of steps that should be taken if exposure to the disease is suspected.

Rabies is a contagious, potentially fatal disease that is transmitted from one infected animal to another (including humans), primarily thorough a scratch or bite. Without prompt medical attention, a person who contracts rabies has little chance of surviving. Prudence therefore dictates that you should suspect exposure whenever you experience a bite or scratch from a wild animal or if an animal's saliva comes into contact with a fresh open wound or a break in your skin. Likewise, if the animal's saliva gets in your eye, you can be infected.

If an incident occurs that causes you to fear exposure, make every effort to secure the suspected animal. This may not be easy to do, but the only way to determine if you have been exposed is to have the animal's brain examined by qualified laboratory personnel. Consequently, in securing the animal an effort should be made to avoid damaging the brain.

Whether or not you are able to secure the suspected animal, you should get yourself promptly to a doctor or hospital for treatment and further guidance. If the animal has been secured and tests subsequently show that it was not rabid, you should have no more problems than you would from any cut or scratch. On the other hand, if the animal is found to have rabies, then you will have to undergo treatment to prevent the development of the disease in your own system.

If the offending animal has not been captured or killed, it is likely that your doctor will recommend these treatments as a precautionary measure. Herein lies the importance of having the animal available for testing; this can avoid the inconvenience and discomfort of unnecessary treatment.

LYME DISEASE

Lyme disease is a bacterial infection that is transmitted by the bite of a tick. In the absence of prompt diagnosis and treatment, Lyme disease can cause serious problems involving the heart, joints, or nervous system. The disease has been known in the U.S. since at least 1975, when an outbreak was diagnosed near Lyme, Connecticut, an event that gave the disease its common name. The frequency of reported Lyme disease cases seems to be increasing, and the geographical range is growing. At present, Pennsylvania is among those states where the disease is most common. Because of variable symptoms -- and sometimes the lack of any symptoms -- the disease is often misdiagnosed.

In this area the tick that spreads Lyme disease is usually the deer tick, a tiny relative of the twice as large and more commonly recognized wood tick. The deer tick can be no bigger than the head of a pin, making it quite inconspicuous; and since its bite is usually painless, the victim is often completely unaware of having been bitten. The deer tick is most active in spring and fall, but it is present in the woods and elsewhere throughout the summer, as well.

Because of the difficulty in diagnosing the disease, it is especially important to take steps to keep from being bitten by a deer tick. It is best to wear long sleeves and pants, and to apply an insect repellent that is effective against deer ticks. After you have been outside, check yourself and any pets carefully for ticks. If any are found, remove them with tweezers by grasping the tick as close as possible to your skin. Gently pull the tick straight out while trying not be squeeze its body. Wash the area of the bite and apply antiseptic.

Symptoms may include a ring-shaped rash, appearing within four to twenty days. Fever, chills, headache, stiffness in joints, weakness and fatigue may also occur. Some cases are without symptoms. If you have any reason to suspect the possibility of Lyme disease, consult a physician promptly. When detected early, the disease usually responds to treatment with antibiotics.

For more information contact the Centers for Disease Control and Prevention at 1888-232-3228 or http://www.cdc.gov

HANTAVIRUS

Hantavirus Pulmonary Syndrome, also known as HPS, is a serious, often deadly, respiratory disease that has been found mostly in rural areas of western United States. The first case of the disease was diagnosed in 1993. The disease is caused by a hantavirus that is carried by rodents and passed on to humans through infected rodent urine, saliva, or droppings. Hantavirus

Pulmonary Syndrome is a rare disease. However, hikers and others who take part in outdoor activities can become exposed to rodent urine, saliva, or droppings and become infected with hantavirus.

The white footed mouse, deer mouse, and cotton rat are carriers of the virus. Hantavirus is spread from wild rodents to people. The virus gets into the air as a mist from urine and saliva, and dust from feces. Breathing in the virus is the most common way of becoming infected; however, you can become infected by touching the mouth or nose after handling contaminated materials. A rodent's bite can also spread the virus.

The virus is not spread from person to person. The virus, which is able to survive in the environment, can be killed by most household disinfectants, such as bleach or alcohol.

Symptoms of HPS usually appear within 2 weeks of infection but can appear as early as 3 days to as late as 6 weeks after infection. First symptoms are general and flu-like: fever (101-104F); headache; abdominal, joint and lower back pain; sometimes nausea and vomiting. However the primary symptom is difficulty in breathing, which is caused by fluid build-up in the lungs and quickly progresses to an inability to breathe. No cure or vaccine is yet available against hantavirus infection. The sooner after infection medical treatment is sought, the better the chance of recovery.

To minimize the risk of infection do not disturb rodents, burrows or dens. Avoid sleeping on bare ground; use a mat. Store food in rodent proof containers and promptly dispose of all garbage. Check potential campsites for rodent droppings and burrows. Sweep and clean out shelters.

For more information contact the Centers for Disease Control and Prevention at 1888-232-3228 or http://www.cdc.gov

UNIFORM DISTRESS SIGNALS

Hikers who find themselves in difficulty while on the trail should utilize the standard method for seeking help. This consists of three short calls audible or visible -- repeated at regular intervals. In daylight a whistle or other audible call, a light flashed with a mirror, or smoke puffs made with a coat and smudge fire may be used. At night a flashlight or three small, bright fires can be substituted.

Such a signal is for emergency used only. Anyone recognizing the signal is honor bound to set about making the rescue at once or to summon more competent aid, since delay may mean disaster. Likewise, the distressed party has an obligation to recompense the rescuers for their time and trouble in extending aid.

Anyone receiving a distress signal should acknowledge it by a signal of two calls, if possible by the same method as that used in the distress call. Whenever practical, local or state police should be notified to avoid duplication of rescue parties.

It is recommended that when hiking, you routinely carry a whistle for use in such emergencies.

TRANSPORTATION

Public transportation to the Appalachian Trail is essentially limited to bus transportation, and then only to a few trailheads. Following is a list of points on the Pennsylvania A.T. where, at last report, scheduled bus service is provided. Because of the frequently changing nature of bus schedules, however, this information is subject to confirmation at your local bus terminal:

Delaware Water Gap
Wind Gap
Palmerton
Port Clinton
Clarks Ferry Bridge (U.S. Rts. 22 & 322)
Duncannon
Caledonia State Park

Trying to arrange a hiking trip through your local bus agent can be a very frustrating experience. You will probably have to start from the beginning and explain exactly where you want to go and why. Then, since most trailheads are not scheduled stops, there will be the matter of helping the agent determine precisely where on the route you want to be let off and/or picked up. Finally, when you actually board the bus, many of the same efforts will have to be expended again in explaining to the driver exactly what is wanted. Patient persistence is called for. Good luck!

DAY HIKES AND SHORT HIKES

There are several areas along the A.T. in Pennsylvania that provide opportunities for day hikes and short backpacking trips utilizing the A.T. side trails, and connecting trails, and connecting trails. These trails are shown on the A.T. maps for Pennsylvania, and many of the important side trails are described in this guide. In addition, these trail systems and hikes using them are described in more detail in the following publications:

Pennsylvania Hiking Trails; Keystone Trails Association: twelfth edition; 1998. Order from KTA, Box 251, Cogan Station, PA 17728-0251.

Circuit Hikes in Virginia, West Virginia, Maryland, and Pennsylvania; The Potomac Appalachian Trail Club. Order from PATC, 118 Park Street, SW, Vienna, VA 22180.

Some areas along the Pennsylvania A.T. that may be of particular interest in the planning of shorter hikes are listed below, along with the identifying Section number in each case:

- The Delaware Water Gap. Section 1
- The Pinnacle, Windsor Furnace, and Hawk Mountain Sanctuary. Section 4.
- Anthony's Wilderness, Game Lands 210 and 211. Section 7.
- Pole Steeple area. Section 12.
- Pine Grove Furnace area. Sections 12 and 13.
- Caledonia State Park area. Section 13.

WEATHER

The weather in Pennsylvania is undependable. A glorious morning can turn sullen within a couple of hours and drench you at lunch. Conversely, more than one fair-weather hiker has risen early for a return to bed, only to find upon arising a second time a couple of hours later that the skies have cleared and the day is a perfect one for the hiking that had been canceled.

In such circumstances, little useful advice can be offered, with one exception. If you hike in Pennsylvania, expect to get rained on and plan accordingly.

Although weather forecasting is a tricky business, and of little value for hike planning purposes more than a day or two in the future, it can usually give you a better than 50-50 chance of knowing what to expect tomorrow. When you are at home, weather forecasts are everywhere. Such is not the case, however, when you are following a hiking trail through remote country. On those infrequent occasions when you do have access to a telephone (and a phone book), if you are overcome with an urge to know tomorrow's weather forecast, there are some possibilities.

Check both the white and yellow pages under "Weather." You may come across a listing there that will give you a recorded weather forecast. A more likely prospect generally, though, is to look in the yellow pages under "Radio Stations" or sometimes "TV/Radio Stations." Often one of the local radio stations will list a number to call or weather and possibly other information. If none of these options pans out, you may want to try calling a radio station even if it lists no weather number. The person who answers the phone may be willing to share with you the next day's weather outlook.

SUMMARY OF DISTANCES

MILES N. to S. (Section)	MILES N. to S. (Cumulative)	Trail Feature	MILES S. to N. (Section)	MILES S. to N. (Cumulative)
		Section 1		
0.0	0.0	I-80, Delaware River Bridge	15.8	228.8
4.8	4.8	Totts Gap	11.0	224.0
6.5	6.5	Kirkridge Shelter	9.3	222.3
7.2	7.2	Fox Gap, Rt. 191	8.6	221.6
8.8	8.8	Wolf Rocks	7.0	220.0
15.8	15.8	Wind Gap	0.0	213.0
		Section 2		
0.0	15.8	Wind Gap	20.7	213.0
4.6	20.4	L.A. Smith Shelter	16.1	208.4
8.1	23.9	Smith Gap	12.6	204.9
15.4	31.2	Little Gap	5.3	197.6
20.7	36.5	Lehigh Gap, Rts 248 & 873	0.0	192.3
		Section 3		
0.0	36.5	Lehigh Gap, Rts 248 & 873	13.3	192.3
0.6	37.1	Outerbridge Shelter	12.7	191.7
5.0	41.5	Lehigh Furnace Gap/Ashfield Rd.	8.3	187.3
7.4	43.9	Bake Oven Knob Shelter	5.9	184.9
8.4	44.9	Bake Oven Knob Road	4.9	183.9
11.5	48.0	New Tripoli Campsite	1.8	180.8
13.3	49.8	Blue Mountain Summit, Rt. 309	0.0	179.0
		Section 4		
0.0	49.8	Blue Mountain Summit, Rt. 309	26.7	179.0
2.2	52.0	Fort Franklin Rd.	24.5	176.8
4.1	53.9	Allentown Shelter	22.6	174.9
5.4	55.2	Tri-County Corner	21.3	173.6
11.5	61.3	Eckville Shelter	15.2	167.5
16.8	66.6	The Pinnacle	9.9	162.2
17.2	67.0	Trail to Blue Rocks Campground	9.5	161.8
20.6	70.4	Windsor Furnace Shelter	6.1	158.4
23.4	73.2	Pocahontas Spring	3.3	155.6
26.7	76.5	Port Clinton, Rt. 61	0.0	152.3

MILES N. to S. (Section)	MILES N. to S. (Cumulative)	Trail Feature	MILES S. to N. (Section)	MILES S. to N. (Cumulative)
		Section 5		
0.0	76.5	Port Clinton, RR Bridge	14.4	152.3
8.6	85.1	Eagles Nest Shelter	5.8	143.7
14.4	90.9	Rt. 183	0.0	137.9
		Section 6		
0.0	90.9	Rt. 183	20.7	137.9
3.6	94.5	Hertlein Campsite	17.1	134.3
6.2	97.1	Round Head/Showers Steps Trail	14.5	131.7
9.3	100.2	Rt. 501 Shelter	11.4	128.6
13.4	104.3	William Penn Shelter	7.3	124.5
20.7	111.6	Swatara Gap	0.0	117.2
		Section 7		
0.0	111.6	Swatara Gap	16.4	117.2
4.8	116.4	Game Land Maintenance Road	11.6	112.4
5.4	117.0	Rausch Gap Shelter	11.0	111.8
10.0	121.6	Yellow Springs Village	6.4	107.2
16.4	128.0	Clarks Valley, Rt. 325	0.0	100.8
		Section 8		
0.0	128.0	Clarks Valley, Rt. 325	16.6	100.8
6.5	134.5	Peters Mountain Shelter	10.1	94.3
7.6	135.6	Fumitory Rocks	9.0	93.2
9.4	137.4	Rt. 225	7.2	91.4
13.3	141.3	Clarks Ferry Shelter	3.3	87.5
16.6	144.6	Clarks Ferry Bridge	0.0	84.2
		Section 9		
0.0	144.6	Clarks Ferry Bridge	14.6	84.2
5.3	149.9	Thelma Marks Memorial Shelter	9.3	78.9
10.3	154.9	Rt. 850	4.3	73.9
12.6	157.2	Darlington Shelter	2.0	71.6
14.6	159.2	Rt. 944	0.0	69.6
		Section 10		
0.0	159.2	Rt. 944	12.3	69.6
4.3	163.5	US Rt. 11	8.0	65.3
10.3	169.5	Rt. 74	2.0	59.3
12.0	171.2	Rt. 174	0.3	57.6
12.3	171.5	Boiling Springs	0.0	57.3

MILES N. to S. (Section)	MILES N. to S. (Cumulative)	Trail Feature	MILES S. to N. (Section)	MILES S. to N. (Cumulative)
		Section 11		
0.0	171.5	Boiling Springs	8.8	57.3
3.0	174.5	Center Point Knob	5.8	54.3
3.9	175.4	Alec Kennedy Shelter	4.9	53.4
6.0	177.5	Whiskey Spring Road	2.8	51.3
8.8	180.3	Rt. 94	0.0	48.5
		Section 12		
0.0	180.3	Rt. 94	10.9	48.5
1.8	182.1	Rt. 34	9.1	46.7
2.8	183.1	Hunters Run Road	8.1	45.7
3.2	183.5	Tagg Run Shelters	7.7	45.3
10.9	191.2	Pine Grove Furnace State Park, Rt. 233	0.0	37.6
		Section 13		
0.0	191.2	Pine Grove Furnace State Park, Rt. 233	19.7	37.6
2.1	193.3	Michaux Road	17.6	35.5
3.4	194.6	Toms Run Shelters	16.3	34.2
8.4	199.6	Arendtsville-Shippensburg Rd.	11.3	29.2
9.6	200.8	Birch Run Shelters	10.1	28.0
12.1	203.3	Milesburn Cabin	7.6	25.5
17.1	208.3	Quarry Gap Shelters	2.6	20.5
19.7	210.9	Caledonia State Park, Rt. 30	0.0	17.9
		Section 14		
0.0	210.9	Caledonia State Park, Rt. 30	17.9	17.9
3.0	213.9	Rocky Mountain Shelters	14.9	14.9
8.3	219.2	Hermitage Cabin	9.6	9.6
9.6	220.5	Tumbling Run Shelters	8.3	8.3
10.8	221.7	Antietam Shelter	7.1	7.1
13.2	224.1	Deer Lick Shelters	4.7	4.7
15.3	226.2	Rt. 16	2.6	2.6
17.9	228.8	Pen Mar	0.0	0.0

WINTER SCENE ON THE TRAIL   © Wayne E. Gross

DETAILED TRAIL DESCRIPTION

SECTION 1

DELAWARE WATER GAP TO WIND GAP

DISTANCE: 15.8 Miles

This section of Trail is maintained from the Delaware River to Fox Gap by the Wilmington Trail Club, and from Fox Gap to Wind Gap by the BATONA Hiking Club.

OVERVIEW OF SECTION 1

From an elevation of 300 ft. at the Delaware River, the trail climbs gradually for 2.7 miles to Mt. Minsi at 1461 ft. with panoramic views of the Delaware River below, Mt. Tammany across the river, and Dunfield Creek where the A.T. ascends the mountain across the river in New Jersey. The trail in the Delaware Water Gap ascends through beautiful hemlock and rhododendron. The trail follows a ridge with slight dips into Totts Gap and Fox Gap and a deeper one into Wind Gap. From early summer on, this whole section is lacking in good springs. Points of interest along the trail are Lake Lenape, Council Rock, Lookout Rock, Mt. Minsi, Lunch Rocks, and Wolf Rocks. In the Wolf Rocks area use care and follow the blazes. The mountain top at this point is nearly one mile wide and the trail once lost, is difficult to find. Wolf Rocks consists of massive jumbled boulders covered with rock tripe and other lichens.

GENERAL INFORMATION

MAPS

Use KTA Section 1 Map or new color KTA Sections 1-6 Map (1998) which shows much trail data. This section of trail is on the following USGS 7 1/2' quads: Stroudsburg, Saylorsburg, and Wind Gap.

ROAD APPROACHES

At some highways the A.T. is marked by an official signboard erected by the Pennsylvania Department of Transportation.

Road approaches to the Trail are as follows:

0.0 mi.　at the Delaware River on the Pennsylvania side of the Interstate 80 bridge cannot be reached from I-80, since even brief parking on the bridge is not possible. Instead, enter Delaware Water Gap village on PA Rt. 611. At the intersection of Main Street and Mountain Road a large PennDOT sign notes the A.T. which comes in from I-80 on Delaware Avenue. This street deadends at the chain barrier on I-80 opposite a red brick highway maintenance building between the toll house and the bridge. A parking lot for hikers is located along the Trail 0.3 miles south of the bridge. See detailed Trail data.

7.2 mi.　from the Delaware River to Fox Gap where PA Rt. 191 crosses between Bangor and Stroudsburg. A small parking area is located here.

15.8 mi. from the Delaware River, in Wind Gap, the Trail
can be reached via the Wind Gap-Saylorsburg Road
which passes under PA Rt. 33. The Trail is visible
from Rt. 33 (a limited access highway) but can be
reached only from the local traffic road. A small
parking area is located adjacent to the A.T. sign.

SHELTERS AND DESIGNATED CAMPSITES

6.5 mi. from the Delaware River is the Kirkridge Shelter.
Water is available in season from an outside tap on
a blue blazed trail toward the Kirkridge Retreat.

PUBLIC ACCOMMODATIONS

In Delaware Water Gap village there are motels, hotels, and
restaurants. The Presbyterian Church of the Mountain,
located just north of the Trail on Main Street, provides a
hostel and information center for hikers. In Wind Gap,
lodging may be obtained at the Gateway Motel, 100 yards
north of the Gap. Water is available for thru hikers.
Lodging and restaurants are located in Wind Gap Borough
down the south side of the mountain.

SUPPLIES

Supplies can be obtained at several places in Delaware
Water Gap Borough. The Pack Shack offers backpacking
equipment and clothing, as well as repair services for
equipment hikers carry. Supplies can be obtained at several
places in Wind Gap Borough.

TRAIL DESCRIPTION

SECTION 1

DELAWARE WATER GAP TO WIND GAP

NORTH TO SOUTH

Miles   Detailed Trail Data

0.0   From the sidewalk on the Pa. side of the Interstate 80 bridge bear left on a path a short distance south of the toll house. This path enters Delaware street. In one block, turn left onto Waring Drive

0.2   Cross Pa. Rt. 611 (Main Street) and continue uphill on Mountain Road.

0.3   Take the next fork to your left and continue on macadam Lake Road.

0.4   Pass hikers parking lot on the right.

0.6   Pass Lake Lenape on the right. A blue blazed side trail on the left reconnects with the A.T. at 0.8 miles.

0.7   Bear left off of gravel road.   The gravel road leads up the mountain and to a side trail to Table Rock with a view of the Water Gap. For the next two miles follow blazes carefully because there are many unmarked trails branching off the A.T.

0.8   Blue blazed side trail to left which reconnects with A.T., at 0.6 miles.

Miles   Detailed Trail Data

0.9   Council Rock. Down the Delaware River, the tilted strata of Mount Tammany on the left side of "The Gap" is said to show the profile of Chief Tammany.

1.5   Cross Eureka Creek and turn left, ascending.

1.7   Lookout Rock. Double back and follow switchbacks carefully along rock faces. At the top of the rocks is a view north to the Pocono Plateau and Big Pocono.

2.4   Panoramic view of the Delaware Water Gap and the surrounding area of Pennsylvania and New Jersey.

2.7   Summit of Mt. Minsi at 1461 ft. Trail follows a gravel road along the crest.

2.8   Trail on the left leads 100 ft to a view south overlooking the Delaware River Valley.

4.4   Turn left onto pipeline right-of-way, then turn right through woods, passing to the south of communications towers.

4.8   Totts Gap. Cross dirt road, trail now ascends over rocks.

4.9   Cross twin power lines with fine views to the north.

5.8   "Lunch Rocks" 50 ft on left with a view north on the ridge into New Jersey.

Miles   Detailed Trail Data

6.4   View south from a clearing at the end of a gravel
         road. Shortly a Blue-blazed trail leads to the
         Kirkridge **SHELTER** with an excellent view to the
         south. **WATER** (seasonal) is available at an outside
         tap toward the Kirkridge Retreat. Follow the blue
         blazed trail.

6.8   Cross orange blazed `trail known as "The Great
         Walk", descends mountain 0.8 miles to a replica of
         an early Celtic Christian Church.

7.1   Bulletin Board at green- blazed cross-trail.

7.2   Arrive at Pa. 191 in Fox Gap. Cross highway, pass
         under power lines and enter old woods road.

7.4   There is a view north to Stroudsburg.

8.1   Trail turns right, joining woods road flanked by
         stone walls.

8.6   Trail turns left after passing under a power line.
         The roadway straight ahead wanders along plateau
         and disappears.

8.8   Reach Wolf Rocks with impressive views to the
         north. Follow the top edge of the rocks before
         turning left. Use care to follow blazes in the next
         5 miles. Once lost, the trail in this area is difficult
         to find.

13.7   Trail crosses a private road of the Blue Mountain
         Water Company affording a view, then meanders
         through varied forest.

14.9   Begin descent into Wind Gap.

<u>Miles</u>   <u>Detailed Trail Data</u>

15.8   Reach intersection with road from borough of Wind
        Gap. To continue on A.T. turn right
        at official Appalachian Trail signboard, passing
        below the overpass carrying Pa. 33, a limited
        access highway.

SECTION 1

WIND GAP TO DELAWARE WATER GAP

SOUTH TO NORTH

<u>Miles</u>   <u>Detailed Trail Data</u>

0.0   At the official Appalachian Trail signboard in Wind
       Gap, ascend steeply from road onto trail through
       woods.

0.9   Reach height of land. Trail meanders through
       varied forest.

2.1   Cross private road of Blue Mountain Water
       Company with view. Continue along ridge top.

6.9   Reach Wolf Rocks with impressive views to the
       north. Trail turns left and drops off the north side
       of the rocks.

7.2   Junction with old roadway. Turn right on roadway
       and pass under power line.

7.7   Trail turns left leaving woods road.

8.4   There is a view north to Stroudsburg.

8.6   Reach Pa. 191 in Fox Gap, crossing directly.

8.7   Bulletin Board at green-blazed cross-trail.

Miles   Detailed Trail Data

9.0   Cross orange-blazed "The Great Walk" which
        descends mountain 0.8 mi. to a replica of an early
        Celtic Christian Church.

9.3   Blue-blazed trail leads to the Kirkridge **SHELTER**
        with an excellent view to the south. **WATER**
        (seasonal) is available at an outside tap toward the
        Kirkridge Retreat. Follow blue blazed trail.

9.4   Cross gravel road. View to the south from a
        clearing

10.0   "Lunch Rocks" 50 ft on right with a view north on
        the ridge into New Jersey.

10.9   Cross two sets of power lines with fine views to
        the north. Descend rocky trail.

11.0   Totts Gap. Trail bears right into woods, passing
        communication towers.

11.3   Turn left on pipeline right-of-way, then turn right
        onto gravel road.

13.0   Trail on the right leads 100 ft to a view south
        overlooking the Delaware River Valley.

13.1   Reach Mount Minsi, 1,461 ft. elevation. Begin
        descent.

13.5   Panoramic view of the Delaware Water Gap and
        the surrounding area of Pennsylvania and New
        Jersey.   For the next two miles follow blazes
        carefully because there are many unmarked trails
        branching off the A.T.

<u>Miles</u>   <u>Detailed Trail Data</u>

14.0   At the top of the rocks is a view north to the
       Pocono Plateau and Big Pocono. Descend
       switchbacks.

14.1   Short trail on the right to Lookout Rock.
       Backtrack and descend.

14.3   Cross Eureka Creek in rhododendron growth.
       Return to edge of escarpment.

14.9   Council Rock. Down river the tilted strata of
       Mount Tammany on the left side of " The Gap " is
       said to show the profile of Chief Tammany.

15.0   Blue-blazed side trail to right reconnects with the
       A.T. at 15.2 miles.

15.1   Reach gravel road.   Turn right downhill. The
       gravel road on the left leads up the mountain and
       to a side trail to Table Rock with a view of the
       Water Gap.

15.2   Pass Lake Lenape on the left. A blue- blazed side
       trail on the right reconnects with the A.T. at 15.0
       miles.

15.4   Pass hikers parking lot on the left and follow Lake
       Drive (dirt road which becomes macadam. Turn
       right and follow Mountain Road downhill.

15.6   Cross Pa. Rt. 611 (Main Street) and continue on
       Waring Drive for 50 ft. Turn right onto Delaware
       Street which deadends in the toll bridge
       maintenance area.

15.8   Reach Pennsylvania end of the Interstate 80
       bridge. To continue on A.T., cross Delaware River
       on this bridge to New Jersey.

SECTION 2

WIND GAP TO LEHIGH GAP

DISTANCE: 20.7 Miles

This section of Trail is maintained by the Delaware Valley Chapter of the Appalachian Mountain Club from Wind Gap to Little Gap, and by the Philadelphia Trail Club from Little Gap to Lehigh Gap.

OVERVIEW OF SECTION 2

The Trail is in State Game Lands most of the way, where overnight camping is permitted. (See introductory section on PA Game Lands.) After climbing out of Wind Gap, and passing Hahn's Lookout, the Trail stays on the ridge crossing Smith Gap until the dip and climb in Little Gap. From there, it traverses an open rocky area which gives impressive, if uninspiring, views of the railroads and Palmerton, industrial home of New Jersey Zinc Company. Close attention to the footway is advised in this area. Be sure to have a canteen of water since springs in the entire section are apt to be dry by early June most years. Part of Blue Mountain north of Lehigh Gap is in the 10 mile diameter Palmerton EPA Superfund Site caused by the zinc smelters that used to operate near Palmerton. The U.S. Public Health Service has advised that hiking this portion of the A.T. does not represent a public health threat.

GENERAL INFORMATION

MAPS

Use KTA Section 2 Map or new color KTA Sections 1-6 Map which shows much trail data. This section of trail is on the following USGS 7.5' quads: Wind Gap, Kunkletown, Palmerton.

ROAD APPROACHES

At some highways the A.T. is marked by an official signboard erected by the Pennsylvania Department of Transportation. Road approaches to the Trail are as follows:

0.0 mi. in Wind Gap the Trail can be seen, but not reached from PA Rt. 33, a limited access highway. The local traffic road, from the village of Wind Gap over the mountain to Saylorsburg, passes under Rt. 33, and it is here in the gap that the Trail crosses. A small parking lot is adjacent

8.1 mi. from Wind Gap, in Smith Gap, a road crosses from Point Phillip to Kunkletown. The road is paved from the north. From the south the gravel road is steep with sharp turns and may be hazardous in snowy conditions. Parking is available at a Game Commission parking lot located 0.3 mi. down the south side of the mountain. NOTE: Reports have been received of vandalism directed at cars parked in the Smith Gap area.

15.4 mi. from Wind Gap, in Little Gap, a road crosses from Danielsville (on PA 946) to the village of Little Gap (or Carbon) on Kunkletown Road. A Game Land parking lot is in the gap.

20.7 mi. from Wind Gap, in Lehigh Gap, the Trail crosses PA
Rt. 248, and then crosses the Lehigh River on PA
Rt. 873 bridge at a point 2 mi. south of Palmerton,
PA. Access is from either end of bridge, with
limited parking at both ends. Additional parking is
available on the old railroad bed above the
highway, accessible from a small entry road east of
the traffic light.

SHELTERS AND DESIGNATED CAMPSITES

4.6 mi. from Wind Gap, on the side trail to Katellen,
0.2 mi. south of the A.T., is the Leroy A.
Smith Shelter, built by the AMC Delaware
Valley Chapter in 1972. Spring is 0.3 mi.
south.

PUBLIC ACCOMMODATIONS

Wind Gap. Lodging may be obtained at the Gateway
Motel, 100 yds. north of the gap. Water is available to thru
hikers.

Palmerton. Two miles upstream, free overnight lodging
with showers is available in the Community Building.
Cooking may be done with stoves outside the building.
Hikers should apply at the Palmerton police station.

Slatington. *Fine Lodging*, 700 Main Street (Pa. Rt. 873),
Slatington, PA 18080-0002. Possibility of hiker pick-up at
Trail; call 610/760-0700. Can be used for mail drop.

Restaurants are available in Wind Gap, Danielsville,
Palmerton, Walnutport, and Slatington.

SUPPLIES

Supplies can be obtained in Wind Gap, Danielsville,
Palmerton, Walnutport, and Slatington.

TRAIL DESCRIPTION

SECTION 2

WIND GAP TO LEHIGH GAP

NORTH TO SOUTH

Miles   Detailed Trail Data

0.0   At a point 0.5 mi. north of Wind Gap village, just
        south of PA Rt. 33, is a parking lot on the east
        side of the local road. Trail crosses road and
        follows it north.

0.1   Pass under PA Rt. 33. Immediately beyond, bear
        left up wood and stone step switchbacks.

0.3   Cross power line. Ascend gradually by
        switchbacks through woods.

0.8   Pass Lookout Rock. Views north over Saylorsburg,
        with Poconos in distance, and Aquashicola Creek
        in Chestnut Valley in foreground. From here, trail
        bears left to traverse the south side of Blue
        Mountain.

1.0   Hahn's Lookout. View south of Wind Gap village
        and South Mountain in the distance.

2.7   Cross underground pipeline.

4.4   Cross transmission line to tower. Good views
        north.

<u>Miles</u> <u>Detailed Trail Data</u>

4.6 Pass blue blazed Katellen Trail on left. AMC's Leroy A. Smith **SHELTER** at 0.14 mi. **SPRINGS** at 0.2, 0.4, and 0.5 mi. Paved road at 0.9 mi.

8.1 Cross Smith Gap Road.

10.6 Pass blue blazed Delps Trail on left (1.1 mi. to road). Very UNRELIABLE **SPRING** 0.3 mi. down side trail.

11.6 Cross powerline.

12.0 Blue blazed trail on the left leads to overlook in 130 yds. NO camping within view of the overlook.

15.1 Weathering Knob. Views north. Trail starts down steep talus slope.

15.4 Cross hard road in Little Gap. To left, 1.5 mi., is Danielsville. Cross pipeline, pass around a locked gate on to old woods road.

15.5 Information board and register. In 100 feet turn left off old road and follow footpath uphill through woods.

16.0 Leave footpath, turn right on old road.

16.6 Cross under high tension wires. Height of land to your left offers superior view.

18.7 Trail bears left off old road into open , rocky area. Views north.

19.3 Turn left at sign. (The Winter Trail, a blue blazed trail, goes straight ahead and rejoins the AT in 1.5 miles in the valley.)

<u>Miles</u> <u>Detailed Trail Data</u>

19.5   Cross a shoulder of the Blue Mountain with fine
       views of the valley. Descend steeply. Cross a
       rocky slide area of the ridge with continuous
       views, but extreme exposure to adverse weather.
       Watch carefully for blazes on rocks.

20.3   Cross old railbed and descend to PA Rt 248. Bear
       left to the traffic light.

20.4   Turn right and cross PA Rt. 248. Turn right along
       road to the bridge.

20.6   Cross to west end of the PA Rt 873 bridge, which
       crosses the Lehigh River.

20.7   At west end, turn right and carefully cross
       highway. Trail will continue up hill.

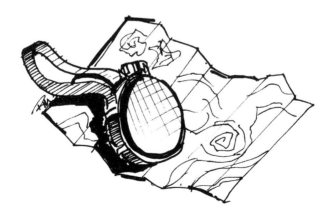

SECTION 2

LEHIGH GAP TO WIND GAP

SOUTH TO NORTH

<u>Miles</u>   <u>Detailed Trail Data</u>

0.0   From west end of PA Rt. 873 highway bridge
        across Lehigh River, cross bridge to east end, then
        turn right along PA Rt. 248.

0.4   Cross PA Rt. 248 at the traffic light, where it
        junctions with PA Rt. 145. Turn left along RT 248
        for 150 feet. Turn right up embankment. Cross
        old railbed.

0.5   At the sign post, begin very steep climb up and
        over the ridge. The, blue blazed, Winter Trail
        continues straight ahead on the railbed and rejoins
        the AT in 1.5 miles. This is a less difficult route.

0.7   Enter open rocky area with no cover for the next
        0.4 miles. Continuous views, but extreme
        exposure to adverse weather. Watch carefully for
        blazes on rocks.

1.1   Cross a shoulder of the Blue Mountain with
        excellent views. Continue to ascend over a rocky
        area.

1.4   Turn right at sign. The blue blazed Winter Trail
        comes in from the left.

1.8   Bear right, as the Trail enters a heavy growth of
        sassafras. This is shortly followed by a rocky area.

<u>Miles</u> <u>Detailed Trail Data</u>

2.0   Open area with views to north. Continue on old
          road.

4.1   Cross under high tension lines. Height of land to
          your right offers superior views.

4.6   Turn left off old road into footpath through the
          woods and begin descent.

5.2   Turn right onto old road. Information board and
          register on left. Pass around locked gate and cross
          pipeline.

5.3   Cross paved road in Little Gap. To the right, 1.5
          mi., is Danielsville. Trail crosses bog, then up
          steep talus slope.

5.6   Weathering Knob. Views north and northwest.

8.6   Blue blazed trail on right leads to overlook in 130
          yds.   NO camping within view of the overlook.

9.0   Cross powerline.

10.1   Pass blue blazed Delps Trail on right (1.1 mi. to
          road). Very UNRELIABLE **SPRING** 0.3 mi. down
          side trail.

12.5   Cross Smith Gap Road.

13.0   Trail turns right on woods road.

16.0   Pass blue blazed Katellen Trail on right. AMC's
          Leroy A. Smith **SHELTER** at 0.14 mi. **SPRINGS** at
          0.2, 0.4, and 0.5 mi. Road at 0.9 mi.

16.2   Fine view north at powerline.

Miles   Detailed Trail Data

17.9   Cross clearing of underground pipeline.

19.6   Pass Hahn's Lookout. View south to Wind Gap
        village and South Mountain in the distance. Trail
        bears right to south side of mountain.

19.9   Lookout Rocks with fine views of the Poconos in
        the distance to the north. In the foreground is
        Chestnut Valley through which flows beautiful
        Aquashicola Creek. Trail descends by
        switchbacks.

20.4   Cross pole line.

20.6   Descend last switchback with stone steps. Pass
        under PA Rt. 33 bridge.

20.7   Cross road to A.T. sign and parking lot.

VIEW FROM BEAR ROCKS © Wayne E. Gross

SECTION 3

LEHIGH GAP TO PA. RT. 309

DISTANCE: 13.3 Miles

This section of the trail is maintained by the Philadelphia Trail Club from Lehigh Gap to Lehigh Furnace Gap; by the Blue Mountain Eagle Climbing Club from Lehigh Furnace Gap to Bake Oven Knob Road; and by the Allentown Hiking Club from Bake Oven Knob Road to Pa. Rt. 309.

OVERVIEW OF SECTION 3

The trail climbs steadily to the Outerbridge Shelter, beyond which the A.T. continues straight ahead, while the blue-blazed North Trail goes to the ridge top. The North Trail is more scenic, but open to winter storms. A point of interest off the North Trail is Devil's Pulpit, overlooking the Lehigh River. The A.T. then passes through Game Lands and dips to Lehigh Furnace Gap. Game Land boundary blazes are often confused with A.T. blazes but are of erratic size and location. USE CAUTION. Climbing again, the trail leads to Bake Oven Knob with its commanding view of fertile farmland below, and its reputation as a birdwatcher's vantage point during the fall hawk migrations. The trail passes Bear Rocks with 360 degree views, and then crosses a knife edge known as "The Cliffs." This is one of the most scenic sections of the A.T. in Pennsylvania.

GENERAL INFORMATION

MAPS

Use KTA Section 3 Map or new color KTA Sections 1-6 Map that shows much trail data. This section of trail is on the following USGS 7 1/2' quads: Palmerton, Lehighton, Slatedale, and New Tripoli.

ROAD APPROACHES

At some highways the A.T. is marked by an official signboard erected by the Pennsylvania Department of Transportation.

Road approaches to the trail are as follows:

0.0 mi.   in Lehigh Gap, this section begins at the west end of the Pa. Rt. 873 bridge over the Lehigh River, two miles below Palmerton. Parking is very limited. (See Section 2.)

5.2 mi.   from Lehigh Gap, access by Ashfield Road between Lehigh Furnace and Ashfield. Parking under transmission lines.

8.4 mi.   from Lehigh Gap, access by Bake Oven Knob Road between Germansville and Andreas. Game Commission parking lot.

13.3 mi. from Lehigh Gap, access by Pa. Rt. 309 at Blue Mountain Summit. There is a Game Commission parking lot just north of the trail where it reaches Pa. Rt. 309 from the north.

SHELTERS AND DESIGNATED CAMPSITES

0.6 mi. from Lehigh Gap is the George W. Outerbridge Shelter, located directly along the trail. Spring is passed before reaching shelter.

7.4 mi. from Lehigh Gap is the Bake Oven Knob shelter, located just south of the trail. Variable springs are located down the hill on a blue-blazed trail at 100 yds. and 200 yds.

PUBLIC ACCOMMODATIONS

Palmerton. Two miles upstream, free overnight lodging with showers is available in the Community Building. Cooking may be done with stoves outside the building. Hikers should apply at the Palmerton police station.

Slatington. *Fine Lodging*, 700 Main Street (Pa. Rt. 873), Slatington, PA 18080-0002. Possibility of hiker pick-up at Trail; call 610/760-0700. Can be used for mail drop. Slatington also has laundromats, banks (with MAC ATM machines), a post office, grocery stores, and 24-hour convenience stores.

Restaurants are also available in Palmerton and Slatington.

SUPPLIES

Supplies can be obtained in nearby Palmerton, Walnutport, Ashfield and Slatington.

TRAIL DESCRIPTION

SECTION 3

LEHIGH GAP TO BLUE MOUNTAIN SUMMIT

NORTH TO SOUTH

<u>Miles</u>   <u>Detailed Trail Data</u>

0.0   At the west end of the Pa. Rt. 873 highway bridge across the Lehigh River, turn right leaving the highway, passing a private driveway on the right. After passing the directional signs, turn right and proceed up the hillside following a gentle switchback. Cross open rocky area. Watch for blazes.

0.2   Pass under power lines. Enter woods.

0.6   Pass piped **SPRING** on right. Reach the George W. Outerbridge **SHELTER** on right. Turn right around shelter, and proceed up the mountain.

0.7   A.T. continues straight ahead, slabbing the southeast side of the mountain. Blue-blazed trail to the right, the North Trail, goes to the top of the mountain and rejoins the A.T. at 2.4 mi. The North Trail is more scenic, but is open to winter storms. It passes another blue-blazed side trail in 0.3 mi., which drops steeply to Devil's Pulpit with good views of the gap. The North Trail, continues on to the ridge, passing a TV tower before rejoining the A.T.

Miles   Detailed Trail Data

2.3   West junction of the AT and the North Trail.
         In this next section the trail passes over the
         Northeast Extension of the Pennsylvania Turnpike,
         which goes through the mountain far below.

4.0   Unmarked trail to rock outcrop on the left. Good
         views. The trail follows State Game Lands
         boundary.

4.7   Trail turns left into State Game Lands.

5.0   Arrive at Ashfield Road, a cross-mountain road
         passable by auto. Trail turns right and descends
         along the road. To the left, along the road 0.7 mi.,
         is a **SPRING**.

5.2   Trail goes left from the road and up under a power
         line into a woods road.

5.4   Trail goes right, leaving woods road.

6.6   Rock outcrop gives winter views to the north.

7.4   Pass Bake Oven Knob **SHELTER** and campsite on
         south side just below the A.T. Blue-blazed trail
         from the shelter leads down hill past an often dry
         SPRING on right and then to a second **SPRING** on
         the right in another 200 yds. This trail continues
         to Bake Oven Knob Road and then to a paved road
         in the valley in 2.0 mi.

7.9   Begin steep rocky ascent of knob.

8.0   Bake Oven Knob, elevation 1,560 ft., site of
         former air beacon. To the left is exceptional
         lookout with 180 degree views to south. To the
         right is view north. Bake Oven Knob is an
         internationally important autumn hawk migration
         observation site.

<u>Miles</u>   <u>Detailed Trail Data</u>

8.4   Cross Game Commission parking lot and Bake Oven
       Knob Road, passable by auto. Continue along
       summit, following a grassy road.

8.8   Turn left where road forks.

9.8   Blue-blazed trail to the right climbs with difficulty to
       Bear Rocks with fine 360-degree views. Don't
       miss it but be careful on the rocks.

10.5   Trail crosses the knife edge known as "The Cliffs"
       with a view to the south.

11.5   A blue-blazed trail to the right descends to base of
       valley in 0.2 mi. to New Tripoli **CAMPSITE** and
       SPRING.   Cross under power line.

13.3   Reach Pa. Rt. 309 at Blue Mountain Summit,
       elevation 1,360 ft. To continue, cross Rt. 309
       directly, then descend on steps. Continue on
       footpath, turning right in 50 yds. Blue blazed trail
       on right 130 ft. before the highway leads to parking
       area.

SECTION 3

BLUE MOUNTAIN SUMMIT TO LEHIGH GAP

SOUTH TO NORTH

Miles Detailed Trail Data

0.0   Pa. Rt. 309, Blue Mountain Summit, elevation
        1,360 ft. In 130 ft. A blue blazed trail on the left
        leads to a parking area.

0.2   Join woods road.

1.8   Beyond the power line the road becomes a trail and
        the footway becomes rocky. A blue-blazed trail to
        the left descends to base of valley in 0.2 mi., and
        then to New Tripoli **CAMPSITE** and **SPRING.**

2.9   Trail turns left, following the knife edge known as
        "The Cliffs" with a view to the south.

3.5   Blue blazed trail to the left climbs with difficulty 50
        yds. to Bear Rocks, with 360 degree views. Don't
        miss it, but be careful on the rocks.

4.5   Bear right on fork at grassy road.

4.9   Reach Bake Oven Knob Road, a cross-mountain
        gravel road passable by autos. Trail passes
        through Game Commission parking lot.

Miles Detailed Trail Data

5.3   Pass over summit of Bake Oven Knob, 1,560 ft.
         elevation. Note remains of old air beacon. To the
         right is exceptional lookout with 180-degree views
         to south. To the left is view north. (Bake Oven
         Knob is an internationally important autumn hawk
         migration observation site.) Reach rock slide on
         north side of mountain. Cross slide using care.

5.9   Bake Oven Knob **SHELTER** and **CAMPSITE** is on
         south side of trail just below A.T. Blue-blazed trail
         leads down past often dry **SPRING** on right, and
         second **SPRING** 200 yds farther down on right.
         Trail then leads 0.7 mi. to Bake Oven Road. It is
         then 1.1 mi. to paved road in valley.

6.7   Winter view to north where trail follows outcrop.

8.1   Cross under transmission line; bear right on
         Ashfield Road for 0.2 mile, a cross-mountain road
         passable by auto.

8.3   At the top of the hill, pass a woods road with gate
         on the left. In 250 feet turn left into the woods on
         the AT.

8.6   Trail turns right following Game Lands boundary
         line.

9.3   Trail turns left, away from Game Lands, and
         passes a large rock outcrop on right. Rough trail to
         top of rocks gives superb views. Cross abandoned
         telephone line. In this next section the trail passes
         over the Northeast Extension of the Pennsylvania
         Turnpike, which goes through the mountain far
         below.

Miles Detailed Trail Data

11.1   Trail junction of blue-blazed North Trail that goes
       to the left for 2.4 mi., and the AT goes straight
       ahead. The North Trail follows the crest of Blue
       Mountain and is the more scenic route, but it is
       open to winter storms. Two miles along the North
       Trail there is another blue blazed side trail leading
       downhill 0.4 mi. to Devil's Pulpit, with good views
       of the Lehigh Gap. The A.T. slabs down the
       southeast side of the mountain. The North Trail
       will eventually rejoin the A.T.

12.6   East junction of the AT and the North Trail.

12.7   Pass George W. Outerbridge **SHELTER** on left.
       A.T. bears left around shelter, passing piped
       SPRING in 105 yds.

13.1   Continue to descend, passing under power lines
       with views into the gap. Please stay on trail.

13.3   Arrive at west end of highway bridge over Lehigh
       River (Pa. Rt. 873). To continue on A.T., cross
       Lehigh River Bridge.

VIEW FROM PULPIT ROCK   © Wayne E. Gross

SECTION 4

PA. RT. 309 TO PORT CLINTON

DISTANCE: 26.7 Miles

This section of the trail is maintained by the Allentown Hiking Club from Pa. 309 to Tri-County Corner and by the Blue Mountain Eagle Climbing Club from Tri-County Corner to Port Clinton.

OVERVIEW OF SECTION 4

From Blue Mountain Summit at Pa. Rt. 309, the trail stays on the ridge, with slight climbs to the Allentown Shelter and at Tri-County Corner. Then a rather sharp descent leads to Eckville. The footway is rocky all the way. Leaving Eckville, the trail climbs gradually and then steeply before leveling out on the ridge leading to the spectacular Pinnacle. A drop again into Windsor Furnace, and another climb precede the steep descent into Port Clinton. Points of interest along the way are Tri-County Corner with its 360-degree views, Dan's Pulpit, The Pinnacle, Pulpit Rock, Windsor Furnace and numerous charcoal hearths, such as the one at Pocohontas Spring. These hearths supplied fuel for the furnace. A special point of interest is the Hawk Mountain Sanctuary near Eckville. This is a world-renowned wildlife refuge, and the first sanctuary in the world to offer protection to birds of prey. The Sanctuary Headquarters Building contains a series of exhibits and is staffed by professional curators who live at the Sanctuary. See the special section in the front of this book for more information about Hawk Mountain Sanctuary.

GENERAL INFORMATION

MAPS

Use KTA Section 4 Map or new color KTA Sections 1-6 Map which shows much trail data. This section of trail is on the following USGS 7 1/2' quads: New Tripoli, New Ringgold, Hamburg, and Auburn.

ROAD APPROACHES

At some highways the A.T. is marked by an official signboard erected by the Pennsylvania Department of Transportation.

Road approaches to the trail are as follows:

0.0 mi. at Pa. Rt. 309 there is a Game Commission parking lot just north of the trail on the east side of the highway.

2.2 mi. from Pa. Rt. 309, access by the Fort Franklin cross-mountain road. This is a rough stone mountain road, which is passable by auto, but better suited to trucks and jeeps. This road can be pinpointed on KTA Section 4 Map. Limited parking.

11.5 mi. from Pa. Rt. 309, in the village of Eckville, the trail crosses Hawk Mountain Road between the villages of Kempton, on Pa. Rt. 143, and Drehersville, on Pa. Rt. 895. This road is the access road to Hawk Mountain Sanctuary. Parking is available at a Game Commission lot on the right side of southbound unimproved Pine Swamp Road, 0.5 mi. from Eckville, and 0.43 mi. from the A.T. on a blue-blazed trail.

25.9 mi. from Pa. Rt. 309, the trail crosses a macadam
         road within sight of Pa. Rt. 61, 0.5 mi. south of
         the village of Port Clinton. Parking is available on
         both sides of the side road. This crossing is
         marked by an official sign erected by the
         Pennsylvania Department of Transportation. The
         trail then proceeds south under Pa. Rt. 61 and
         along the Schuylkill River.

A ten-car parking area is located just south of Port Clinton
along Route 61. It is accessible only from the southbound
lane. It connects to the A.T. via a blue blazed trail.

SHELTERS AND DESIGNATED CAMPSITES

4.1 mi. from Blue Mountain Summit is the Allentown
         Hiking Club Shelter. A spring is nearby.

11.5 mi. from Blue Mountain summit is the Eckville Shelter
         (0.2 mi. south on the road).   In season has a port-
         a-potty and caretaker present. Water is also
         available from a faucet at the side of the
         caretaker's house when the caretaker is present.

20.6 mi. from Blue Mountain Summit is the Windsor
         Furnace Shelter. A spring and outhouse are
         nearby. Limited camping is permitted around the
         shelter. Another campsite for tenters has been
         established nearby. See detailed trail data for
         directions.

26.5 mi. In Port Clinton, follow blue-blazed trail 0.4 mile
         north on Penn Street to the town pavilion.

PUBLIC ACCOMMODATIONS

Overnight or weekend lodging is available for hikers at the Y.W.C.A. Blue Mountain Camp, Hamburg, Pa. DONATION REQUESTED. Meals are available during the camp season, usually June 9 through the end of August. At other times of the year, prior arrangement must be made with the camp caretaker by calling 610/562-8691 or writing to Camp Director, YWCA, 8th & Washington Sts., Reading, Pa. 19601. The camp is one mile south of the A.T. on a blue-blazed side trail from Pocohontas Spring.

The Port Clinton Hotel, 0.5 mi. north of the trail on Pa. Rt. 61, provides lodging for hikers. Accommodations and restaurants are available in Hamburg, Pa., three miles south of Port Clinton on Pa. Rt. 61.

Blue Rocks Campground (1.5 mi. down yellow-blazed trail at 18.5 mi. from Blue Mountain Summit; 9.9 mi.from Port Clinton) offers camping, hot showers, laundry facilities, and a camp store.

SUPPLIES

Supplies can be purchased in Hamburg, Pa. There are no grocery stores in either Eckville or Port Clinton.

TRAIL DESCRIPTION

SECTION 4

BLUE MOUNTAIN SUMMIT TO PORT CLINTON

NORTH TO SOUTH

Miles	Detailed Trail Data
0.0	From the east side of Rt. 309 at Blue Mountain Summit, cross road directly, descend on steps and continue on footpath turning right in 50 yards.
0.4	Trail turns left leaving footpath and continues on a Game Commission road.
1.8	Bear left off Game Commission road, trail becomes a footpath.
2.2	Reach Fort Franklin road, passable by auto. Cross road and continue on a woods road.
3.8	Blue-blazed trail leads to spring in 375 feet, and leads on to the Allentown Shelter. A.T. turns sharp right up eroded woods road. Spring may be dry by mid-summer, but water can always be found by following the yellow-blazed trail 1,100 feet down the south side of the mountain to a spring.
4.1	Blue-blazed trail to left leads in 30 yds. to the Allentown **SHELTER**. The privy is 200 feet west of shelter.
4.3	Turn left off woods road. Trail becomes rocky.

Miles   Detailed Trail Data

5.3   A blue-blazed trail leads left, down the Old Dresher
        Road, not passable for autos, 1.8 mi. to the valley
        floor. The A.T. turns right upgrade on the Old
        Dresher Road.

5.4   Reach Tri-County Corner. A blue-blazed trail to the
        right leads a short distance to the top of the rock
        pile where a marker indicates the intersection of
        Berks, Lehigh, and Schuylkill Counties. Excellent
        views. Tri-County Corner is the place where, in
        1926, construction was first begun on the
        Appalachian Trail in Pennsylvania by a work party
        from the Blue Mountain Eagle Climbing Club.

5.5   Turn left off woods road.

6.4   Balanced Rock on left. Good views.

7.4   Blue-blazed trail to the left leads steeply downhill
        115 yds. to Dan's **SPRING**, not dependable.

8.0   Blue-blazed trail to left leads 1.9 mi. into the
        valley, passing **SPRING** at 3/4 mi.

8.6   A few feet to the left of the trail is Dan's Pulpit,
        named in honor of Daniel K. Hoch, one of the
        founders of the Blue Mountain Eagle Climbing
        Club.

9.2   Turn left on old woods road.

9.7   A.T. turns sharp left down the mountain on an old
        road. A blue-blazed trail to the right leads 2 mi. to
        Hawk Mountain Sanctuary's North Lookout, and
        then to the headquarters and museum. A fee is
        charged to hike in the sanctuary. **NO CAMPING IS
        PERMITTED**.

Miles   Detailed Trail Data

10.0   Turn right off old road onto footpath.

11.2   Turn right, then left, and come to log walkway and
        bridge over swamp and creek. Bear left, then
        sharp right.

11.3   Turn right on old logging road.

11.5   Cross hard surfaced Hawk Mountain Road. Right
        leads to Hawk Mountain Sanctuary; left to Eckville
        and Eckville **SHELTER** in 0.2 miles by following
        blue blazes along road to shelter.

11.7   Crossing of woods roads. Turn left.

12.4   Bear right off woods road onto Game Commission
        service road. Old A.T. is now a blue-blazed trail to
        Game Lands parking lot, 0.43 mi.

13.3   Unmarked Panther **SPRING**, always running, on
        right.

13.6   A.T. turns left up the mountain on woods road

        *EXCEPT AS NOTED IN THIS GUIDE, NO CAMPING
        OR FIRES ARE ALLOWED IN THIS AREA WHICH IS
        THE HAMBURG BOROUGH WATERSHED.*

14.2   Blue blazed woods road on right leads to the A.T.
        at Windsor Furnace in 1.5 miles.

14.8   Reliable Gold **SPRING** 30 yds. on right. <u>No
        camping or fires</u>.

15.1   Keep left where blue blazed woods road goes right.

Miles   Detailed Trail Data

16.8   Blue-blazed trail to the left leads 80 yds to the
        spectacular Pinnacle, 1,635 ft. elevation. This is
        considered by many to be <u>the most spectacular
        vista</u> along the A.T. in Pennsylvania. There are
        two caves below the Pinnacle, and many sheer
        cliffs to explore. A.T. turns sharply to the right.
        There is a trail register on tree at the vista. **NO
        CAMPING OR FIRES ALLOWED**.

17.2   Yellow-blazed trail to the left leads down a steep
        hill for 1.3 mi. to Blue Rocks. In another 0.2 mi. is
        the Blue Rocks Campground, privately owned,
        where **SUPPLIES** can be purchased at the camp
        store.

18.4   Pass through cleft in rock formation.

18.5   Rock field 10 yds to the right

18.8   Excellent view to the left on a rock outcropping.
        Pass tower on right.

19.0   Pulpit rock on the left at 1,582 ft. elevation, with
        excellent views of the Pinnacle to the left and Blue
        Rocks in the foreground. Begin steep descent.

        **NO CAMPING OR FIRES ALLOWED
        EXCEPT AS NOTED IN THIS GUIDE.**

19.2   Trail bears left descending mountain on an old
        woods road.

19.5   Blue blazed trail on left leads to Blue Rocks
        Campground.

20.6   Trail to the right leads 500 ft. to the Windsor
        Furnace **SHELTER**. Limited camping permitted
        around the shelter.

Miles   Detailed Trail Data

20.7   Trail, now on a gravel road, crosses Furnace Creek. Do NOT swim or bathe in creek.

20.8   Arrive at trail sign and Windsor Furnace, site of an early pig iron works. Note glassy slag in the footpath. The remains of the old engine foundation are in the undergrowth. An essential ingredient was charcoal, and the trail passes many flat round charcoal hearths, or burning sites, 30 to 50 ft. in diameter.

The Borough of Hamburg has provided **CAMPSITES** 0.5 mile south on a blue-blazed trail along a service road. The sites are located beyond the Reservoir buildings and parking area on a dirt road to the left. Water may be obtained from the stream at the campsites. The campsites are accessible by vehicles.

NO OTHER CAMPING IS ALLOWED EXCEPT AS NOTED.

The A.T. goes left on an old woods road.

21.4   Take right fork from woods road. Use care.

21.6   Intermittent **STREAM**, dry in summer.

22.2   Minnehaha **SPRING, frequently dry**.

23.4   Pocohontas **SPRING**, good all year. A blue-blazed trail to the left leads 1 mi. to the YWCA Blue Mountain Camp.

24.3   Cross clearing for former telephone line.

24.4   Cross Game Lands boundary line.

Miles   Detailed Trail Data

25.3   Begin descent to Port Clinton.

25.9   Road crossing and parking area. Angle left across
and descend embankment.

26.0   Turn right under Pa. Rt. 61 highway bridge. Bear
right along Schuylkill River.

26.4   Turn right away from the river. Blue blazed trail on
right leads 100 yds to parking area.

26.5   Turn left on Broad St. and cross Little Schuylkill
River.   Ahead 0.4 mile is a pavilion with water and
pit toilet which hikers may use, follow blue blazes.

26.7   Turn left and cross Schuylkill River on railroad
bridge. Parking on Port Clinton streets is limited.
Use area east of Pa. Rt. 61, 0.5 mi. south of
village.

SECTION 4

PORT CLINTON TO BLUE MOUNTAIN SUMMIT

SOUTH TO NORTH

<u>Miles</u>   <u>Detailed Trail Data</u>

0.0   Cross the Schuylkill River on a railroad bridge.

0.1   Reach Broad St. in Port Clinton and turn right.
Limited parking on streets. Use area east of Pa.
Rt. 61, 0.5 mi. south of village.

0.2   Turn right on Penn St. and then bear right into
woods along Schuylkill River. To the left 0.4 mile
is a pavilion with water and pit toilet which hikers
may use, follow blue blazes.

0.7   Bear left and cross under Pa. Rt. 61.

0.8   Cross macadam side road at parking area and begin
ascent.

1.1   Switchbacks to the right.

1.4   Reach top of ridge.

2.4   Cross Game Lands boundary. Be careful to
continue straight ahead on trail.

2.5   Cross clearing for former telephone line.

3.1   Bear right and descend from ridge.

3.3   Pocohontas **SPRING**. A blue-blazed trail to the
right leads 1.0 mi. to the YWCA Blue Mountain
Camp.

Miles   Detailed Trail Data

3.5   Bear left where road forks.

4.5   Pass Minnehaha **SPRING**, frequently dry.

5.9   Enter lands of the Hamburg Borough Watershed.

**NO FIRES OR CAMPING ALLOWED
EXCEPT AS NOTED IN THIS GUIDE.**

Arrive at trail sign and the site of Windsor Furnace,
an early pig iron works. Note glassy slag in the
footpath. The remains of the old engine foundation
are in the undergrowth. An essential ingredient
was charcoal, and the trail passes many flat round
charcoal hearths, or burning sites, 30 to 50 ft. in
diameter. A blue-blazed trail to the right follows
service road 0.5 mile to a **CAMPSITE** provided by
the Hamburg Water Authority. Sites are located
beyond the buildings and parking area on a dirt
road to the left. WATER may be obtained at the
stream behind the campsites. Campsites are
accessible to vehicles.

*EXCEPT AS NOTED, THIS IS THE ONLY
CAMPING PERMITTED IN THE WATERSHED. NO
SWIMMING IS PERMITTED IN THE CREEK OR IN
THE IMPOUNDMENT.*

A.T. goes straight ahead.

6.0   Trail, now on a road, crosses Furnace Creek and
bears right onto a woods road. **NO SWIMMING OR
BATHING PERMITTED.**

<u>Miles</u>   <u>Detailed Trail Data</u>

6.2   Turn right where a trail to the left leads 500 ft. to
        the Windsor Furnace **SHELTER**. Limited camping
        permitted around shelter.

7.2   Blue blazed trail on the right leads to Blue Rocks
        Campground.

6.3   Trail ascends Blue Mountain gradually, then
        steeply.

7.7   Pulpit Rock, elevation 1,582 ft. Excellent view of
        the Pinnacle to the left, with Blue Rocks in the
        foreground. **NO CAMPING OR FIRES ALLOWED**.

7.9   Pass tower and service road on left.

8.3   Rock field 10 yds. to the left. Pass through cleft in
        rock formation.

9.5   Yellow-blazed trail to the right leads down a steep
        hill for 1.3 mi. to Blue Rocks. In another 0.2 mi. is
        the Blue Rocks Campground, privately owned,
        where **SUPPLIES** can be purchased.

9.9   Blue-blazed side trail to the right leads 80 yds. to
        the spectacular Pinnacle, 1,635 ft elevation. This is
        considered by many to be <u>the most spectacular
        vista</u> along the A.T. in Pennsylvania. There are two
        caves, and many sheer cliffs to explore. There is a
        trail register on a tree at the vista. A.T. turns
        sharply to the left. **NO CAMPING OR FIRES
        ALLOWED**.

11.6   Keep right where blue blazed woods road goes left
        to Furnace Creek.

11.9   Reliable Gold **SPRING** 30 yds on left. <u>NO
        CAMPING OR FIRES</u>.

<u>Miles</u>   <u>Detailed Trail Data</u>

12.5   Junction of trails. A.T. turns right toward Eckville.
        Blue blazed woods road goes left to rejoin A.T. in
        1.5 miles.

12.9   Reach crest in hemlock trees. Disregard the white
        boundary blazes of the Game Lands. Trail turns
        left descending.

13.6   Bear right, disregarding grassy woods road to the
        left. Pass Panther **SPRING** on the left. Continue
        descending on the old Windsor Furnace Road
        through Game Lands.

14.4   Bear left off road. Old A.T. is now a blue-blazed
        trail to the Game Lands parking lot, 0.43 mi.

15.2   Cross hard surfaced Hawk Mountain Road. Right
        leads to Eckville and Eckville Shelter in 0.2 miles
        by following blue blazes along road to the shelter.
        To left leads to Hawk Mountain Sanctuary, a very
        desirable side trip. **NO CAMPING PERMITTED AT
        THE SANCTUARY**.

15.4   Left on old logging road.

15.6   Left off road, then sharp right. Come to bridge and
        walkway over creek and swamp. After swamp,
        turn right, then left.

16.7   Turn left onto abandoned cross-mountain road,
        climbing to the ridge.

17.0   Blue-blazed trail to the left leads 2 mi. to Hawk
        Mountain's North Lookout. A fee is charged to
        hike in the Sanctuary. **NO CAMPING PERMITTED
        AT THE SANCTUARY**.

Miles   Detailed Trail Data

17.5   Leave old mountain road and turn right on foot
        trail.

18.1   Pass rock outcrop known as Dan's Pulpit where
        hiking's grand old man, Danny Hoch, conducted
        Sunday services. Fine views at 1,600 ft.
        elevation.

18.8   Blue-blazed trail to right leads 1.9 mi. into the
        valley, passing **SPRING** at 3/4 mi.

19.4   Blue-blazed trail to the right leads steeply downhill
        115 yds. to Dan's **SPRING**. May be dry in dry
        weather.

20.3   Balanced Rock to the right of trail. Fine views.

21.3   Blue blazed trail on left to Tri-County Corner, the
        site of the very first blazing of the Appalachian
        Trail in Pennsylvania, in 1926, by a crew from the
        Blue Mountain Eagle Climbing Club. Trail to the
        left leads 400 ft. to the top of the rock pile where
        there is a marker denoting the intersection of
        Berks, Lehigh, and Schuylkill Counties. Excellent
        views.

21.4   A.T. turns left. Trail becomes very rocky. Blue-
        blazed trail straight ahead on the Old Dresher Road
        leads 1.8 mi. into the valley.

22.5   Turn right onto woods road.

<u>Miles</u>   <u>Detailed Trail Data</u>

22.6   Blue-blazed trail to the right leads 30 yds. to the
        Allentown Hiking Club **SHELTER** for six. This blue
        trail leads another 1,200 yds. to a **SPRING**, and
        then turns left connecting with the A.T. in 375 ft.
        The spring may be dry by mid-summer, but water
        can always be found by following the yellow-
        blazed trail 1,100 ft. down the mountain to
        another spring.

22.9   Blue blazed trail from the spring rejoins the A.T.

24.6   Cross Fort Franklin road, passable by auto.

24.8   Bear left, leaving woods road, trail becomes a
        footpath.

25.0   Footpath ends, trail turns right onto wood road.

26.4   Bear right onto footpath

26.7   Reach Pa. Rt. 309, Blue Mountain Summit. To
        continue north, cautiously cross Pa. Rt. 309 and
        reenter woods on footpath.

SECTION 5

PORT CLINTON TO PA. RT. 183

DISTANCE: 14.4 Miles

This section of the trail is maintained by the Blue Mountain Eagle Climbing Club.

OVERVIEW OF SECTION 5

The trail begins with a steep climb out of Port Clinton, gaining 1,000 feet in two miles. The footway is quite rocky for most of the first six miles. Beyond, the trail passes through a maturing forest that is surprisingly rock-free, and altogether pleasant hiking. The Game Commission administrative road, over which the trail was previously routed, is crossed twice before reaching Pa. Rt. 183.

GENERAL INFORMATION

<u>MAPS</u>
Use KTA Section 5 Map or new color KTA Sections 1-6 Map that shows much trail data. This section of trail is on the following USGS 7 1/2' quads: Auburn and Friedensburg

ROAD APPROACHES

At some highways the A.T. is marked by an official signboard erected by the Pennsylvania Department of Transportation.

Road approaches to the trail are as follows:

0.0 mi. Parking is available on a side road that starts east of Pa. Rt. 61, 0.5 mi. south of the town of Port Clinton, 0.8 mi. from the parking area at the south end of the Schuylkill Railroad bridge to the west of Pa. Rt. 61 in Port Clinton. The bridge is 0.1 mi. from the Canal Museum.

A ten-car parking area is located just south of Port Clinton along Route 61. It is accessible only from the southbound lane. The parking connects to the A.T. via a blue blazed trail.

14.4 mi. from Port Clinton, the trail crosses Pa. Rt. 183 between Strausstown and Summit Station. There is a Game Commission parking lot 0.3 mi. south of the mountaintop on the east side of the road.

SHELTERS AND DESIGNATED CAMPSITES

0.0 mi. In Port Clinton, follow blue-blazed trail 0.4 mile north on Penn Street to the town pavilion. Water is available from people from the church.

8.6 mi. from Port Clinton is Eagles Nest Shelter for eight. Yeich Spring is nearby.

Camping is permitted in this section since almost all of the Trail is in Game Lands, but Game Commission camping regulations as outlined previously must be followed.

PUBLIC ACCOMMODATIONS

In Port Clinton is the Port Clinton Hotel where hikers can secure lodging. The Peanut Shop provides snacks. In Shartlesville there are several famous eating places serving family style meals. In Hamburg there are hotels and motels.

SUPPLIES

There are grocery stores in Hamburg, three miles south of Port Clinton, and in Shartlesville.

TRAIL DESCRIPTION

SECTION 5

PORT CLINTON TO PA. RT. 183

NORTH TO SOUTH

Miles   Detailed Trail Data

0.0   Cross the Schuylkill River on the railroad/driveway bridge. Continue along driveway and turn right across tracks.

0.1   Climb steep bank to old single railroad bed. Continue left on track for 175 ft. Turn right uphill ascending very steeply for the next 0.5 mile.

1.0   Cross old pipeline.

1.4   Cross new pipeline.

1.5   Come to Dynamite Road. A.T. turns sharp right here. Footway becomes rocky. Trail on left leads to Mountain Road at the foot of the ridge.

2.0   Cross Game Lands road.

2.4   Come to Game Lands road. Follow road to the right (but do not cross) for about 45 yds. and re-enter woods.

2.5   Reach Auburn Lookout, a rock outcrop off the trail to the right. Excellent view of Auburn village and surrounding area.

<u>Miles</u>   <u>Detailed Trail Data</u>

3.1   Cross Marshalls Path. Blue-blazed trail to the left
        leads to Mountain Road in Bellmans Gap at the
        foot of the ridge.

3.3   Come to Game Lands road. Cross diagonally,
        following arrows, cairns, and blazes for about 120
        yds. Enter woods on trail that is now south of the
        road.

4.0   Pass unmarked Phillip's Canyon **SPRING** trail on
        the left. Spring is 135 yds down a steep descent
        and is <u>sometimes dry</u>. Spring is at a stoned
        enclosure.

5.2   Come to Game Lands road. Cross directly,
        following arrows, cairns and blazes for about 100
        yds. Trail enters woods and is now on the north
        side of the road. Soon begin descent from the
        ridge on rock steps.

5.7   At bottom of ridge turn left. Follow trail with
        improved footway through the woods.

6.1   A.T. bears right.

6.7   Cross old mountain road. To the left are Game
        lands parking lot, 1.6 mi., and Shartlesville, 3.6 mi.

8.6   Come to blue-blazed trail that leads in 0.3 mi. to
        Eagles Nest **SHELTER** , 0.2 mile to Yeich **SPRING**,
        and 0.4 mile to vista.   Cross Game Lands
        boundary, leaving Weiser State Forest.

8.8   Cross Game Commission Administrative Road.
        Continue on trail.

9.3   Cross blue blazed Sand Spring Trail. Sand **SPRING**,
        a fine walled spring is located 0.14 mi. to the left.
        NO CAMPING is permitted at or near the spring.

<u>Miles</u>   <u>Detailed Trail Data</u>

10.4   Reach junction with Eagles Nest Trail. Eagles Nest
        vista is 1.16 miles to the left. Game Commission
        Road is 0.41 mile to the right. A.T. continues
        across junction.

12.0   Cross small stream.

13.1   Blue-blazed trail to left leads 300 yds. to Black
        Swatara **SPRING**. <u>NO CAMPING.</u>

13.9   Cross Game Commission administrative road.
        Game Lands parking lot is to the left at the foot of
        this road and adjacent to Pa. Rt. 183.

14.0   Turn left onto woods road.

14.4   Pass Rentschler marker, 15 yds to the right,
        erected in honor of Dr. H. F. Rentschler, who,
        beginning in 1926, led the work parties which
        originally established the A.T. between the Lehigh
        and Susquehanna Rivers. Reach Pa. Rt. 183.

        To continue on A.T., cross Pa. Rt. 183 directly.

SECTION 5

PA. RT. 183 TO PORT CLINTON

SOUTH TO NORTH

Miles   Detailed Trail Data

0.0   Trail crosses Pa. Rt. 183 at official PennDOT
       highway sign marking the A.T. Trail follows road
       up slight incline and immediately passes Rentschler
       marker, 15 yds off to the left. Dr. H. F. Rentschler
       led the work parties which, beginning in 1926,
       originally established the A.T. between the Lehigh
       and Susquehanna Rivers. Trail continues on woods
       road.

0.4   Leave woods road, turning right onto trail.

0.5   Cross Game Lands road that comes uphill from
       right. Parking lot is located 0.2 mi. to the right
       adjacent to Pa. Rt. 183.

1.3   Blue-blazed trail to the right leads 200 yds. to
       Black Swatara **SPRING**.

2.4   Cross small stream.

3.8   Leave obscure Game Lands road, and enter woods
       to the left.

4.0   Reach junction with Eagles Nest Trail. Eagles Nest
       vista is 1.16 miles to the right. Game Commission
       Road is 0.41 mile to the left. A.T. continues
       across junction.

Miles   Detailed Trail Data

5.1   Cross blue blazed Sand Spring Trail. Sand **SPRING**,
        a fine walled spring is located 300 yds. to the
        right. <u>No camping</u> at or near the spring.

5.6   Cross Game Commission Administrative Road.

5.8   Cross Game Lands boundary and enter Weiser
        State Forest. Blue-blazed trail leads left 0.3 mi. to
        Eagle Nest **SHELTER**, 0.2 mile to Yeich **SPRING**,
        and 0.4 mile to vista.

7.7   Meet old cross mountain road. To the right in 1.6
        mi. is Game Lands parking lot and Shartlesville, 2.0
        mi. further.

8.3   Bear left on old A.T.

8.7   Turn sharp right and start ascent of ridge on rock
        steps.

9.2   Just beyond the top of the ridge, come to Game
        Lands road. Cross directly, following arrows,
        cairns, and blazes for about 100 yds. Enter woods
        on trail now south of road. Footway becomes
        rocky.

10.4   Pass Phillip's Canyon **SPRING** Trail to the right.
        Spring is 135 yds on left after a steep descent.
        <u>Variable</u>.

11.1   Come to Game Lands road. Cross diagonally
        following arrows, cairns and blazes for about 120
        yds. Enter woods on trail, now north of road.

11.3   Cross Marshalls Path, a well - worn blue-blazed
        trail from Bellmans Gap, which leads to hard-
        surfaced Mountain Road at foot of ridge.

Miles   Detailed Trail Data

12.0   Reach Auburn Lookout, a rock outcrop to the left, off trail. Excellent view of the village and surrounding area.

12.1   Come to Game Lands road. Follow road for about 45 yds. Do not cross. Re-enter woods.

12.4   Cross Game Lands road.

12.9   Come to Dynamite Road, a trail leading on right to Mountain Road at the foot of the ridge. A.T. turns sharp left here.

13.0   Cross new pipeline.

13.4   Cross old pipeline. Shortly after, start descent of ridge, gradually at first, then steeply.

14.3   Come to old railroad bed. Turn left for 60 yds. then descend bank on right via path to railroad tracks. Cross tracks to paved driveway.

14.4   Reach railroad bridge over Schuylkill River and end of section. Turn right on Broad St. in Port Clinton. Parking is limited in the borough; use area on side road east of Pa. Rt. 61, 0.5 mi. south of the borough.

SECTION 6

PA. RT. 183 TO SWATARA GAP

DISTANCE: 20.7 Miles

This section of the trail is maintained by the Blue Mountain Eagle Climbing Club.

OVERVIEW OF SECTION 6

Except for a slight dip in Shuberts Gap, the trail stays on the ridge until the final descent into Swatara Gap. Points of interest along the way is the site of Fort Dietrich Snyder (1756), one of a chain of forts and blockhouses built as protection from the Indians; Showers Steps, 500 rough stone steps forming a path down the point of Round Head, built by Lloyd Showers; and Pilger Ruh Spring, a colonial watering stop.

GENERAL INFORMATION

MAPS

Use KTA Section 6 Map or new color KTA Sections 1-6 Map that shows much trail data. This section of trail is on the following USGS 7 1/2' quads: Friedensburg, Swatara Hill, Pine Grove, Fredericksburg, Indiantown Gap.

ROAD APPROACHES

At some highways the A.T. is marked by an official signboard erected by the Pennsylvania Department of Transportation.

Road approaches to the trail are as follows:

0.0 mi. at Pa. Rt. 183 the trail crosses between Strausstown and Summit Station. There is a Game Commission parking lot 0.3 mi. south of the mountaintop on the east side of the road.

9.3 mi. from Pa. Rt. 183, trail crosses Pa. Rt. 501 between Bethel and Pine Grove. There is parking just north of the crossing.

11.3 mi. from Pa. Rt. 183, trail crosses Pa. Rt. 645 between Frystown and Pine Grove. Parking on the west side of the road.

20.7 mi. from Pa. Rt. 183, in Swatara Gap, access is by Pa. Rt. 72, just south of the Interstate 81 overpass. No access from Interstate 81. Pa. Rt. 72 goes north from the village of Lickdale at the intersection where Pa. Rt. 72 turns. No designated parking.

SHELTERS AND DESIGNATED CAMPSITES

3.7 mi.   Hertlein Campsite is located in Shuberts Gap.
          Springs are available.

8.8 mi.   Applebee Campsite is located near Pilger Ruh
          (Pilgrims Rest) Spring.

9.3 mi.   from Pa. Rt. 183 is the Rt. 501 Shelter: fully
          enclosed, water, port-a-potty (in season). There is
          a caretaker year-round.

13.4 mi. from Pa. Rt. 183 is the William Penn Shelter, a
          new two-story structure with two sleeping levels.
          The second level is a loft with windows.

SUPPLIES

The Woods Creek store and restaurant is located 0.8 mi.
south of A.T. in Swatara Gap along Pa. Rt. 72; hikers
welcome.   There are convenience stores in the village of
Lickdale 2.4 miles south along PA Rt 72.

TRAIL DESCRIPTION

SECTION 6

PA. RT. 183 TO SWATARA GAP

NORTH TO SOUTH

Miles   Detailed Trail Data

0.0   At the official Pennsylvania Department of
Transportation signboard, cross the highway to the
west side; go up a slight bank and follow signs and
blazes across large open field on an old road
leading to the former Shuberts Summit cross-
mountain road.

0.3   Turn sharp right and in 100 yds. reach historical
marker for Fort Dietrich Snyder. (See chapter on
history.)   A.T. turns sharp left at marker. Blue-
blazed trail ahead leads to a **SPRING** in 0.13 mi.
which can be reached by going north on the cross-
mountain road for 125 yds. Turn left across a
clearing to reach spring in the woods.

2.9   Cross oil pipeline.

3.6   Arrive in Shuberts Gap. Two tent platforms are
located here. A blue-blazed trail to the left leads
downhill to a dam and pond. The water is very
cold. Below the dam is private property; do not
trespass.

3.7   Brook and **SPRINGS** at the Hertlein **CAMPSITE**.
Cross brook. A Trail register box is on a tree.

Miles   Detailed Trail Data

3.9   Trail turns left onto relocation.

4.1   Reach Shikellamy Summit, a fine lookout.

5.2   Reach a charcoal hearth on right.

6.2   Reach Round Head and Showers Steps and a great
        viewpoint. A.T. turns sharp right uphill. Lloyd
        Showers, an early trail worker, constructed a path
        of 500 rough stone steps down the face of Round
        Head. This blue-blazed path continues through the
        Kessel (Kettle) and rejoins the A.T. At the base of
        Showers Steps is a **SPRING**. South on the A.T. in
        200 feet is the Shanaman Marker. William F.
        Shanaman was mayor of Reading, Pa. and an early
        trail worker.

6.3   An unmarked trail to left leads100 ft. to unnamed
        lookout. Great view of the Kessel and north to
        Second and Sharp Mountains.

6.8   A.T. turns left.

7.4   Blue-blazed Kessel Trail on left descends steeply
        over a talus slope with a view to the south.

8.8   Blue-blazed trail to the left leads to Pilger Ruh
        (Pilgrims Rest) **SPRING**, a watering stop dating
        back to colonial times. Camping is permitted a
        short distance to the right of the junction of the
        A.T. and the side trail at Applebee **CAMPSITE**.

9.3   Reach Pa. Rt. 501. Watch for signs to Rt. 501
        SHELTER, 0.16 mi. on blue-blazed trail. Cross
        highway directly.

Miles   Detailed Trail Data

9.4   Descend to Kimmel Lookout, an outstanding
       viewpoint named for Richard Kimmel, a trail worker
       for over 40 years, and an honorary member of
       ATC.

9.5   Cross buried cable line clearing; turn left and tnen
       right along edge of the mountain.

11.2   Reach Pa. Rt. 645 at site of radio tower. Cross
       highway directly and enter woods.

13.4   Blue-blazed trail to the right leads to Blue Mountain
       SPRING, 125 yds downhill. Blue-blazed trail to left
       leads 0.12 mi. to William Penn **SHELTER** that
       includes a loft with windows.

14.6   Cross oil pipeline, continuing on old stage road. To
       the left in 200 yds. is a tri-county marker denoting
       the intersection of Berks, Lebanon and Schuylkill
       Counties.

16.1   Turn left onto obscure abandoned power line.
       Then turn right in 20 yds. View over Monroe
       Valley is to the left.

17.4   Dip into hollow passing the old charcoal road
       leading downhill to the left into Monroe Valley.

18.3   The white-blazed Game Lands boundary and the
       A.T. run together at this point. Use caution.

19.3   After descending gradually on the point of the
       ridge, make a sharp right and begin descending the
       mountain on the north side.

19.9   Cross woods road.

<u>Miles</u>   <u>Detailed Trail Data</u>

20.1   Approaching the fence along Interstate 81, turn
        left; follow blazes along and near fence. Do not
        cross the fence. Look for **SPRING**.

20.3   Turn right, passing under I-81 bridges. Turn right
        onto Old State Road along the Swatara Creek.

20.6   Turn left and cross Swatara Creek on "Waterville
        Bridge," a historic iron bridge.

20.7   Reach Pa. Rt. 72. A.T. crosses highway.

SECTION 6

SWATARA GAP TO PA. RT. 183

SOUTH TO NORTH

<u>Miles</u>	<u>Detailed Trail Data</u>
0.0	Cross Pa. Rt. 72; cross Swatara Creek on "Waterville Bridge," a historic iron bridge..
0.1	Turn left, then right, onto hard-surfaced Old State Road along Swatara Creek
0.4	Turn sharp left uphill under Interstate 81 bridges. Turn left, then keep to the right of the fence in the woods. Look for **SPRING**.
0.6	Turn right away from fence.
0.7	Cross woods road. Trail now ascending.
1.3	Cross circle of old charcoal hearth.
1.4	Reach crest of mountain. Trail turns left.
2.2	Use caution as confusing white Game Lands boundary blazes run with the A.T. blazes.
3.3	Trail to the right leads down to Monroe Valley.
4.7	Reach obscure abandoned power line cut. View of Monroe Valley is to the right

Miles   Detailed Trail Data

6.1   Cross oil pipeline, continuing on old stage road. To
          the right in 200 yds. is a tri-county marker
          denoting the intersection of Berks, Lebanon and
          Schuylkill Counties.

7.3   Blue-blazed trail leads left 225 yds. to Blue
          Mountain **SPRING**. Blue-blazed trail to right leads
          in 0.1 mi. to William Penn **SHELTER** that includes a
          loft with windows.

9.5   Cross Pa. Rt. 645 between Frystown and Pine
          Grove. Pass tower. Trail continues along ridge.

11.2   Trail turns left, then right, crossing buried cable
          line and descending to Kimmel Lookout. This
          lookout is named for Dick Kimmel, a trail worker
          for more than 40 years, and an honorary member
          of the ATC.

11.4   Reach Pa. Rt. 501 and cross highway directly.
          Watch for signs to Rt. 501 **SHELTER**, 0.16 mi. on
          blue blazed trail.

11.8   Blue-blazed trail to the right leads to Pilger Ruh
          (Pilgrims Rest) **SPRING**, a watering stop dating
          from colonial times. Camping is permitted a short
          distance to the left of the junction of the side trail
          and the A.T. at Applebee **CAMPSITE**.

13.2   Blue-blazed Kessel Trail on the right with view to
          the south.

13.9   A.T. turns right.

Miles   Detailed Trail Data

14.4   An unmarked trail to right leads 100 ft. to
        unnamed lookout. Great view of the Kessel and
        north to Second and Sharp Mountains.

14.5   Pass the Shanaman Marker and reach Round Head
        with excellent views. William F. Shanaman was
        mayor of Reading, Pa. and an early trail worker.
        A blue-blazed trail leads to Showers Steps. Lloyd
        Showers, an early trail worker, constructed a path
        of 500 rough stone steps down the face of Round
        Head. The blue-blazed trail circles back to rejoin
        the A.T. A **SPRING** is at the foot of the steps.

16.6   Shikellamy Summit, a fine lookout.

17.0   Cross brook and reach the **SPRINGS** at the Hertlein
        CAMPSITE. A trail register is on a tree.

17.1   Shuberts Gap with two tent platforms. A blue-
        blazed trail leads downhill to a dam. Water is very
        cold. Below the dam is private property; do not
        trespass.

17.8   Cross oil pipeline.

20.4   Reach Shuberts Summit abandoned cross-mountain
        road. A.T. turns right for 100 yds., then left onto
        a woods road. A marker indicates the site of Fort
        Dietrich Snyder (1756), one of a chain of forts
        erected as protection against Indian Raids. A blue-
        blazed trail to the left leads 0.13 mi. to a **SPRING**.

20.7   Reach Pa. Rt. 183. To continue on the A.T., cross
        highway and follow woods road.

SECTION 7

SWATARA GAP TO CLARKS VALLEY

DISTANCE: 16.4 Miles

This section of the trail is maintained by the Blue Mountain Eagle Climbing Club from Swatara Gap to Rausch Gap, and by the Brandywine Valley Outing Club from Rausch Gap to PA RT 325.

OVERVIEW OF SECTION 7

The first 1.3 miles are on public roads, a condition that will change with pending relocation. Watch for blazes. After leaving the roads, the trail climbs Second Mountain, then descends into Stony Creek Valley and enters St. Anthony's Wilderness, the largest roadless tract in southeastern Pennsylvania. Historic Rausch Gap village is directly on the trail. An exploration of the area will reveal building foundations, a cemetery, old hand dug wells, abandoned railroad beds, railroad facilities, and other remains of a once thriving industrial community. (See the chapter on history.) The trail goes through Rausch Gap, then ascends Sharp Mountain and Stony Mountain before dropping into Clarks Valley. In addition to Rausch Gap Village and Yellow Springs Village (a long abandoned coal mining community), a point of interest is the northern terminus of the Horse-Shoe Trail on top of Sharp Mountain. During times when the trees are not in leaf it is possible from Stony Mountain to see DeHart Dam and the Harrisburg Water Supply Reservoir.

GENERAL INFORMATION

MAPS

Use KTA Section 7 Map or color KTA Sections 7 & 8 Map (1996) which shows much trail data. This section of trail is on the following USGS 7 1/2' quads: Tower City, Indiantown Gap, Grantville, and Enders.

ROAD APPROACHES

At some highways the A.T. is marked by an official signboard erected by the Pennsylvania Department of Transportation.

Road approaches to the trail are as follows:

0.0 mi. in Swatara Gap, access is by PA Route 72, just north of the Interstate 81 overpass. Limited parking. No access from Interstate 81. There is limited parking along these roads. A new State Park is planned for this area and when construction begins parking areas may be designated by signs. Parking may be arranged at the Bashore Boy Scout Reservation, 0.9 mi. west of the A.T. at intersection of Pa. Rt. 443 and Ridge Road, by advance permission of the Camp Director, 630 Janet Ave., Lancaster, Pa. 17601.

1.4 mi. from Swatara Gap, where the A.T. meets and then follows Pa. Rt. 443, is a small parking lot on state park property.

16.4 mi. from Swatara Gap, where the A.T. crosses Pa. Rt.
    325 in Clarks Valley, there is a Game Commission
    parking lot. This trail crossing is located 10.1 mi.
    east of the intersection of Pa. Rt. 325 and Pa. Rt.
    225, 2.0 mi. north of the village of Dauphin.

SHELTERS AND DESIGNATED CAMPSITES

5.4 mi. from Swatara Gap, in Rausch Gap, the Rausch Gap
    Shelter has a reliable spring and outhouse facilities.
    This shelter was built in 1972 by the Blue
    Mountain Eagle Climbing Club with the permission
    of the Pa. Game Commission. No camping or fires
    are permitted elsewhere except as authorized. This
    shelter is for the use of through hikers only. The
    area is patrolled by Game Commission Officers,
    who enforce all regulations.

PUBLIC ACCOMMODATIONS

The Bashore Boy Scout Reservation may be used by hiking
groups if advance arrangements are made with the Camp
Director, Camp Bashore, Lancaster-Lebanon Boy Scout
Council Office, 630 Janet Ave., Lancaster, Pa. 17601.

Parking for three cars north side of Second Mountain. For
information, phone 717/397-0851 or 717/865-4045.

SUPPLIES

There are convenience stores in the village of Lickdale,
approximately 2.2 miles south of the A.T. along Route 72.
At 1.9 mi. from Swatara Gap directly on the trail is a phone
booth.

TRAIL DESCRIPTION

SECTION 7

SWATARA GAP TO CLARKS VALLEY

NORTH TO SOUTH

Miles	Detailed Trail Data
0.0	From west side of PA Route 72 begin gradual uphill. A new State Park will be constructed in the Swatara Gap area. During the construction of the dam and new highways, the Trail may be temporarily relocated from time to time. Use caution and be alert for changes.
0.9	Reach open field; turn left.
1.4	Reach PA Rt. 443 and small parking lot; turn left.
1.5	Pass road on right.
1.9	Pass telephone booth on right.
2.0	Turn right onto a macadam road (Ridge Road).
2.5	Bear right onto a dirt road leading into a housing development. Stay on road
2.7	Turn left onto a woods road between two houses. Stay on trail. Do not trespass.
2.9	Enter Pa. Game Lands. No camping or fires are permitted except as authorized. (See section on Game Lands.)

Miles   Detailed Trail Data

3.1   Pass a woods road on left.

3.3   Turn left uphill. A **SPRING** beside the trail may be
         dry in late summer.

3.7   Reach the crest of Second Mountain. Turn left and
         begin a gradual descent on the old wagon road.
         Unblazed middle patch path leads straight down
         the north side of the mountain. Pink-blazed trail on
         the left leads to an overlook at a boulder field in
         1.5 miles.

4.5   Cross Haystack Creek on a wooden footbridge.

4.7   Reach the center of the ruins of Rausch Gap
         Village. The Community well is on the left of the
         square. Do not build fires or camp here in violation
         of Game Commission regulations.

4.8   Reach the old railroad bed of the Susquehanna and
         Schuylkill Railroad, now a Game Commission
         administrative road. About 150 ft. to the right are
         the remains of the turntable pit. Across the road
         from the turntable pit is the site of the Rausch Gap
         Station. To the right the maintenance road leads
         3.6 mi. to Gold Mine Road and a Game
         Commission parking lot. To the left the road leads
         to the Cold Spring Trail, 4.5 mi. to the site of the
         former Cold Spring Station, and 14.0 mi. to
         Ellendale Forge and another Game Commission
         parking lot. The A.T. turns left here, crossing
         Rausch Creek on the old stone-arch railroad bridge.

5.0   Turn right and follow old mine road uphill. Use
         care in following blazes through old mining area.
         Orange-blazed trail goes left along an old road and
         leads to a Game Commission parking lot at Cold
         Spring in 2.8 miles.

Miles   Detailed Trail Data

5.4   Blue-blazed trail to the left leads to Rausch Gap
         SHELTER and **SPRING**. An orange-blazed trail
         leads right along Rausch Creek and past stone
         ruins.

5.5   Red-blazed Old Stage Trail goes right, crosses
         Rausch Creek, and proceeds east to the Gold Mine
         area.

5.6   Pass old open-cut strip mine on left, with Rausch
         Creek on right shortly after trail turns toward the
         left. The trail will now follow an old stage road for
         the next 7.0 mi.

7.7   Bear right at a small clearing and continue on old
         stage road at the junction of the Cold Spring Trail,
         which leads left downhill 0.9 mi. to the Game
         Commission administrative road.

7.9   Junction with the blue-blazed Sand Spring Trail on
         the right, which leads up and over Stony Mountain
         to Rt. 325 in 1.5 miles.

10.0   Pass through the ruins of Yellow Springs Village.
         The Blue-blazed side trail to the right leads 0.7 mi.
         to the site of a stone tower and an old mine
         entrance. From there it goes left about 100 yards
         to a loading ramp area for the inclined plane.   It
         then turns left about 0.75 mi. back to the A.T. The
         trail at the site of Yellow Springs Village continues
         straight through the village site, then along a creek
         bed.

10.2   Junction with blue-blazed Yellow Springs Trail in a
         narrow ravine where water may be found.

10.4   Proceed uphill on old stage road.

Miles   Detailed Trail Data

12.6   Turn sharp right off stage road onto a woods trail.
        The stage road continues straight ahead,
        descending to the ruins of Rattling Run village and
        the Horseshoe Trail.

12.7   Cross Rattling Run on stepping stones in
        rhododendron grove.

13.3   Reach the summit of Stony Mountain and the site
        of a dismantled fire tower. The trail descends to
        Clarks Valley on the old fire tower road.

13.4   This is the northern terminus of the HorseShoe
        Trail, marked by a monument stone. The
        HorseShoe Trail leads left downhill, then on to
        Valley Forge, PA, a total of 137 miles. For more
        information about the HorseShoe Trail, write to:
        HorseShoe Trail Club, PO Box 182, Birchrunville,
        PA 19421

16.1   Red blazed Henry Knauber Trail leads left very
        steeply up the mountain and reaches the
        HorseShoe Trail in 1.6 miles. **SPRING** on right
        along the A.T.

16.3   Blue blazed Water Tank Trail leads left along a dirt
        road.

16.4   Cross Clarks Creek and reach the Game
        Commission parking lot and Pa. Rt. 325.

SECTION 7

CLARKS VALLEY TO SWATARA GAP

SOUTH TO NORTH

<u>Miles</u>   <u>Detailed Trail Data</u>

0.0   From Pa. Rt. 325 trail crosses the Game
       Commission parking area, onto a woods road and
       crosses Clarks Creek.

0.1   Blue blazed Water Tank Trail leads right along dirt
       road.

0.3   Red blazed Henry Knauber Trail leads right very
       steeply up the mountain and reaches the
       HorseShoe Trail in 1.6 miles. **SPRING** on right
       along the A.T.

3.0   Reach the northern terminus of the HorseShoe
       Trail, marked by a monument stone. The
       HorseShoe Trail goes to the right downhill, then on
       to Valley Forge, PA, a total of 137 miles. For more
       information write to: HorseShoe Trail Club (See
       north-to-south).

3.1   Reach the summit of Stony Mountain and the site
       of dismantled fire tower. A.T. becomes a woods
       trail.

3.7   Cross Rattling Run on stepping stones in
       rhododendron grove.

3.8   A.T. turns left onto an old stage road, which the
       trail follows for 7.0 mi.

Miles   Detailed Trail Data

6.2   Junction with blue-blazed Yellow Springs Trail in a
         narrow ravine where water may be found.

6.4   Pass through the ruins of Yellow Springs Village.
         The Blue-blazed side trail to the left leads 0.7 mi.
         to the site of a stone tower and an old mine
         entrance. From there it goes left about 100 yards
         to a loading ramp area for the inclined plane.   It
         then turns left about 0.75 mi. back to the A.T. The
         trail at the site of Yellow Springs Village continues
         straight through the village site, then along a creek
         bed.

8.5   Junction with the blue-blazed Sand Spring Trail on
         the left, which leads up and over Stony Mountain
         to Rt. 325 in 1.5 miles.

8.7   Junction with the Cold Spring Trail, which leads
         right downhill 0.9 mi. to the Game Commission
         administrative road. A.T. bears left.

10.8   Trail turns right, leaving the old stage road. Pass a
         large open-cut strip mine on the right, with Rausch
         Creek on the left.

10.9   Red-blazed Old Stage Trail goes left, crosses
         Rausch Creek, and proceeds east to the Gold Mine
         area.

11.0   Blue-blazed trail to the right leads to the Rausch
         Gap **SHELTER** and **SPRING**. An orange-blazed trail
         leads right along Rausch Creek and past stone
         ruins.

11.4   Trail turns left onto the cinder administrative road
         of the Game Commission. This road is the former
         road bed of the Susquehanna and Schuylkill
         Railroad, which ceased operations in the 1940's.

Miles Detailed Trail Data

11.6 Cross Rausch Creek on an old stone arch railroad bridge. Directly after crossing the creek, turn right onto a woods road. The Game Commission road continues 3.6 mi. to the Gold Mine Road and Game Commission parking lot. An old turntable pit is 150 ft. ahead to the right of the road. Across the road from the turntable pit is the site of the Rausch Gap station.

11.7 Pass through the ruins of the Rausch Gap Village. The Community well is on the left of the square. Do not build fires or camp here in violation of Game Commission regulations.

11.8 Trail bears right where road forks.

11.9 Cross Haystack Creek on wooden foot bridge and begin ascending Second Mountain.

12.7 Reach the crest of Second Mountain and turn right, descending. Pink-blazed trail on the right leads to an overlook at a boulder field in 1.5 miles.

13.1 Pass **SPRING** that may be dry in late summer on left of trail and then turn right on old woods road.

13.3 Pass a woods road coming in from right.

13.5 Leave Pa. Game Lands and enter private property. Pass between two houses. Stay on trail. Do not trespass.

13.7 Turn right onto a well-used dirt road. Descend hill; cross small stream. Stay on road.

13.9 Turn left onto a macadam road (Ridge Road).

14.4 Turn left onto Pa. Rt. 443.

Miles   Detailed Trail Data

14.5   Pass telephone booth on left.

14.9   Pass road on left. A new State Park will be constructed in the Swatara Gap area. During the construction of the dam and new highways, the Trail may be temporarily relocated from time to time. Use caution and be alert for changes.

15.0   Turn right, leaving PA Rt. 443 at small parking lot and going along fence row in open field.

15.5   Turn right, entering woods. Start gradual uphill.

16.4   Reach Pa. Rt. 72. End of this section.

ROCKY RIDGE   © Wayne E. Gross

SECTION 8

CLARKS VALLEY TO SUSQUEHANNA RIVER

DISTANCE: 16.6 Miles

This section of the trail is maintained from PA RT. 325 to Pa. RT. 225 by the Susquehanna Appalachian Trail Club, and from Pa. Rt. 225 to the Susquehanna River by the York Hiking Club.

OVERVIEW OF SECTION 8

After the initial climb to the crest of Peters Mountain, made easier with construction of a large swichback in 1992 the trail stays on the ridge top with only minor changes in elevation until the descent to the Susquehanna River. This descent is gradual, making use of switchbacks to reach the railroad and the highway beyond.

Points of interest along the trail include Shikellimy overlook, Table Rock overlook, many large rock outcrops, and excellent views up and down the Susquehanna River. The Juniata River can be seen to the north, and to the south is the Rockville Bridge, the longest stone arch railroad bridge in the world. This bridge, built in 1902, carries Conrail's mainline tracks across the Susquehanna River. It also carried the A.T. until 1955.

Fumitory Rocks are named for the climbing fumitory, *Adlumia fungosa*, which grows there. Also known as Allegheny vine and mountain fringe, this member of the poppy family is found on the moist ledges of wooded mountain sides from Canada to North Carolina. The vines of the plant grow up to 12 feet long, and the flowers bloom generally in early July in this latitude. Pennsylvania's Fumitory Rocks are said to be the only place along the Appalachian Trail where this plant is found.

GENERAL INFORMATION

MAPS

Use KTA Section 8 Map or color KTA Sections 7 & 8 Map (1996) which shows much trail data. This section of trail is on the following USGS 7 1/2' quads: Enders, Halifax, and Duncannon.

ROAD APPROACHES

At some highways the A.T. is marked by an official signboard erected by the Pennsylvania Department of Transportation.

Road approaches to the trail are as follows:

0.0 mi. in Clarks Valley, the A.T. crosses Pa. Rt. 325 10.1 mi. east of the intersection of Pa. Rt. 325 and Pa. Rt. 225 which is 2.0 mi. north of the Village of Dauphin. A Game Lands parking lot is located at the trail crossing.

9.4 mi. from Clarks Valley, the A.T. crosses Pa. Rt. 225 at the crest of Peters Mountain. Parking on east side of highway. The Parking lot is out of sight from highway. Take gravel road uphill approximately 200 feet to parking lot on left. An information bulletin is at the parking lot.

16.0 mi. from Clarks Valley, the A.T. crosses U.S. Rts. 22 & 322 at the east end of the Clarks Ferry Bridge. Adequate parking along the river, adjacent to the highway. An information bulletin board is at the base of the mountain.

16.6 mi.from Clarks Valley, at the west end of the Clarks Ferry Bridge along U.S. Rts. 22 & 322, is limited parking.

SHELTERS AND DESIGNATED CAMPSITES

6.5 mi. from Clarks Valley is the Peters Mountain Shelter. Spring is located 275 yds. down a steep blue-blazed trail on the north side of the mountain. The shelter was constructed in 1993.

13.3 mi. from Clarks Valley is the Clarks Ferry Shelter. Good spring.

PUBLIC ACCOMMODATIONS

Just beyond the west end of the Clarks Ferry Bridge, in the Village of Amity Hall, are two motels and a restaurant. The town of Duncannon, through which the trail passes, is 0.6 mi. south of this section. Duncannon offers lodging and restaurants.

SUPPLIES

There are no opportunities to purchase supplies on this section of the trail. Supplies may be purchased in Duncannon.

TRAIL DESCRIPTION

SECTION 8

CLARKS VALLEY TO SUSQUEHANNA RIVER

NORTH TO SOUTH

<u>Miles</u>	<u>Detailed Trail Data</u>
0.0	Cross Pa. Rt. 325, entering the woods in Pa. Game Lands, and begin ascent of Peters Mountain.
0.4	Blue-blazed trail to the left leads 100 yds to a **SPRING**.
0.6	Continue ascent on switchback to right.
0.9	Reach the crest of Peters Mountain. Trail turns left along the crest.
2.5	Blue-blazed Shikellimy Trail to the left leads down the mountain 0.9 mi. to PA Rt. 325. A.T. continues along ridge.
3.2	Bear left, climbing Shikellimy Rocks with winter views overlooking Clarks Valley.
3.9	Blue-blazed trail to the left leads to viewpoint at a small cliff in 60 yds with good views of Clarks Valley.
5.6	Bear left on an abandoned cross-mountain road. This road leads right to Powells Valley and the village of Enterline.

<u>Miles</u>   <u>Detailed Trail Data</u>

5.7   A.T. turns right up the mountain. Blue-blazed
        Victoria Trail continues 1.5 mi. on the left to PA
        Rt. 325 near the site of the Victoria Furnace, a
        Revolutionary War era iron furnace. Note: Victoria
        Trail may be moved farther north on A.T. in near
        future pending Game Commission approval.

6.5   Reach the Peters Mountain **SHELTER**. Water is
        found at a **SPRING** located 275 yds. down a blue-
        blazed trail on the north side of the mountain.
        Water is difficult to obtain at this site. Large new
        shelter and privy was finished in fall, 1994.

7.3   Yellow-blazed trail to the right leads in 1.5 mi. to
        Camp Hebron, a church camp. Use of camp trails
        is by permission only; a fee is charged.

7.4   Table Rock, 15 yds to the left on blue-blazed trail
        with a good view to the south.

7.6   Pass over Fumitory Rocks. (See note under
        "Overview of Section 8" at the beginning of this
        Section.)

8.0   Outlook to the south on left along an unmarked
        path.

8.8   Pass under double power lines with excellent views
        to the north. Trail follows dirt road from here to
        PA Rt. 225.

9.2   Pass a radio facility of the Pennsylvania Fish and
        Boat Commission on your left.

Miles   **Detailed Trail Data**

9.4   Reach parking area with information bulletin board,
        then cross PA Rt. 225 diagonally downhill to the
        left, and in 45 yds. turn right up a steep bank.
        CAUTION: Cross highway quickly since there is
        very limited sight distance along the highway.

9.7   Reach access road to a microwave tower.

9.8   Leave the access road to the right and follow the
        crest of the mountain to the tower.

10.2   Pass to the right of the Bell Telephone relay tower.
        A.T. then crosses a pipeline right-of-way with
        limited views before entering the woods and
        continuing straight along the ridge.

11.4   Bailey Geodetic Survey marker to the left.

12.1   Cross another pipeline with good views south to
        Dauphin Gap, Rockville Railroad Bridge, and
        Harrisburg.

12.3   Pass a rock overhang that could be used as an
        emergency shelter.

13.0   Cross under the power line. From the crest there
        are excellent views of the Rockville Bridge to the
        south and the Juniata and Susquehanna Rivers to
        the north.   After leaving the powerline clearing,
        continue along the ridgetop before descending
        onto a bench on the south face of the mountain.

13.3   Blue-blazed side trail to the left leads 300 ft. to the
        Clarks Ferry **SHELTER**, and 600 ft. to a reliable
        piped **SPRING**.

Miles   Detailed Trail Data

13.6   The Trail reaches the crest of the mountain, with blue-blazed Susquehanna Trail to the right that rejoins the A.T. at 15.6 miles. The blue trail is 1.0 mile long and has a steep, rocky descent off the ridge.

14.3   Former powerline with views north and south.

14.6   Reach point of mountain after passing rock outcroppings. Begin descent via large switchbacks.

15.0   Blue-blazed trail on right leads 60 yds to a **SPRING**.

15.1   View of Sherman's Creek and town of Duncannon across the Susquehanna River.

15.2   Reach a logging road and follow it a short distance; turn left and descend a short distance before turning right. After a short distance, cross an intermittent stream; pass an old stone foundation for a mule barn to the right. This was part of the Berkeheimer Farm, which burned sometime between 1910 and 1920. Trail follows gentle bench on the mountain.

15.6   Junction with blue-blazed, Susquehanna Trail on right. Begin steady descent to highway and railroad tracks.

16.0   After crossing the <u>active</u> railroad tracks, the trail turns left to the east end of the Clarks Ferry Bridge. Turn right and cross the highway with care; proceed along pedestrian walkway on south side of bridge. CAUTION: Trains approach at fast speed with no warning.

16.6   Reach the west end of the bridge.

SECTION 8

SUSQUEHANNA RIVER TO CLARKS VALLEY

SOUTH TO NORTH

Miles	Detailed Trail Data

0.0   Begin section at the west end of the Clarks Ferry Bridge. Cross the bridge on the pedestrian walkway.

0.6   At the east end of the bridge cross the highway with care. Turn left at the A.T. sign. Walk 100 yards along the road, turn right and cross an <u>active</u> railroad track (CAUTION: Trains approach at fast speed with no warning) and climb end of stone retaining wall. Begin ascent of ridge.

1.0   The trail levels and follows the bench edge to the southwest. To the left is the blue-blazed Susquehanna Trail that rejoins the A.T. at 3.0 mi.

1.3   To the left is an old stone foundation for a mule barn that was part of the Berkeheimer Farm, which burned between 1910 and 1920. Shortly after passing the foundation, the trail crosses an intermittent stream. After a short distance, the trail bears left up the mountain.

1.4   Reach another woods road. Turn right and follow the road to the end. The trail continues up to the point of the mountain.

1.6   Blue-blazed trail on left leads 60 yds to a **SPRING**.

Miles   Detailed Trail Data

1.5   View of Shermans Creek and the town of
         Duncannon across the Susquehanna River. The
         trail switches back at the viewpoint and continues
         climbing to the crest of the mountain by large
         switchbacks to rock outcroppings at the top.

2.0   The trail follows the crest to the east through
         wooded areas and over rock outcroppings that
         offer good views to the north and south.

2.3   Former power line with views north and south.

3.0   The Susquehanna Trail, a blue-blazed side trail,
         goes straight ahead and rejoins the A.T. at 1.0
         mile. This trail is 1.0 mile long and has a steep,
         rocky descent of the ridge. The A.T. leaves the
         crest to a bench on the south face of the
         mountain, passing through some mountain laurel
         on the bench.

3.3   Blue-blazed side trail leads 300 ft. to the Clarks
         Ferry **SHELTER**, and 600 ft. to a reliable piped
         SPRING.

3.6   The trail regains the mountain crest after passing
         the side trail. After a short distance, it crosses
         under the power line. From the crest there are
         excellent views of the Rockville Bridge to the
         south, and the Juniata and Susquehanna Rivers to
         the north. (Watch for rattlesnakes at this
         viewpoint.) The trail follows an old woods road for
         about 400 yds.

4.3   Pass a rock overhang that could be used as an
         emergency shelter.

4.5   Cross a pipeline with good views south to Dauphin
         Gap, the Rockville Railroad Bridge, and Harrisburg.

Miles   Detailed Trail Data

5.2   Bailey Geodetic Survey marker to the right.

6.4   The A.T. leaves the woods and crosses another
       pipeline right-of-way before passing to the left of a
       Bell Telephone relay tower. The trail re-enters the
       woods and continues along the ridge.

6.8   Reach the access road to a microwave tower and
       turn left.

6.9   The trail leaves the access road to the left.

7.2   Cross PA Rt. 225 diagonally uphill. Bear right on a
       dirt road leading to trailhead parking area.
       CAUTION: Cross highway quickly since there is
       very limited sight distance along the highway.

7.4   Pass a radio facility of the Pennsylvania Fish and
       Boat Commission on the right.

7.8   Pass under double power line with excellent views
       to the north. The trail follows a dirt road from here
       to PA Rt. 225.

8.6   Overlook to the south on right along an unmarked
       path.

8.9   Pass over Fumitory Rocks. (See note under
       "Overview of Section 8" at the beginning of this
       Section.)

9.2   Table Rock, 15 yds to the right on blue-blazed trail
       with a good view to the south.

9.5   Yellow-blazed trail to the left leads 1.5 mi. to
       Camp Hebron, a church camp. Use of camp trails
       is by permission only, a fee is charged.

Miles   Detailed Trail Data

10.1   Arrive at the Peters Mountain **SHELTER**. Water is
        found at a **SPRING** located 275 yds down a blue-
        blazed trail on the north side of the mountain.
        Water is difficult to obtain at this site. Large new
        shelter and privy was finished in Fall, 1994.

10.9   Blue-blazed Victoria Trail leads downhill to the
        right, reaching PA Rt. 325 in 1.5 mi. To the left,
        this cross-mountain road leads to Powells Valley
        and the Village of Enterline. Note: Victoria Trail
        may be moved farther north on A.T. in the near
        future pending Game Commission approval.

11.0   Bear right off abandoned cross-mountain road.
        This road leads left to Powells Valley and the
        village of Enterline.

12.7   Blue-blazed trail to the right leads to viewpoint at a
        small cliff in 60 yds with good views of Clarks
        Valley.

13.4   Trail bears right and climbs onto Shikellimy Rocks
        with winter views overlooking Clarks Valley.

14.1   Blue-blazed Shikellimy Trail to the right leads down
        the mountain 0.9 mi. to PA Rt. 325. A.T.
        continues along ridge.

15.7   A.T. turns right, leaving ridge line and begin
        descent on a long switchback.

16.0   End of switchback, turn left downhill.

16.2   Blue-blazed trail to the right leads 100 yds to a
        SPRING.

<u>Miles</u>   <u>Detailed Trail Data</u>

16.6   Reach Pa. 325. Across the highway is a large
       Game Lands parking area. This is the end of this
       section.

SECTION 9

SUSQUEHANNA RIVER TO PA 944

DISTANCE: 14.6 Miles

This section of the Trail is maintained by the Mountain Club of Maryland from the Susquehanna River to the Darlington Trail, and by the Cumberland Valley Appalachian Trail Management Association from the Darlington Trail to Route 944.

OVERVIEW OF SECTION 9

From the west end of the Clarks Ferry Bridge the first two miles are on paved roads through the town of Duncannon. A steep climb up Cove Mountain ends at Hawk Rock with outstanding views. The Trail then stays on the ridge, through the woods with rocky footing. Good views are available at the pipeline before the Trail descends to cross PA Rt. 850, followed by the climb and descent of Little Mountain and the climb and descent of Blue Mountain before reaching PA Rt. 944. Points of interest are Hawk Rock and the Darlington Shelter, a prefabricated shelter with no piece weighing more than 80 pounds. At the crest of Blue Mountain, the trail intersects the Darlington Trail and the Tuscarora Trail which is blue blazed.

GENERAL INFORMATION

MAPS

Use KTA Sections 9 & 10 black and white map or color Map #1, "Cumberland Valley," published by the Potomac Appalachian Trail Club.

ROAD APPROACHES

At some highways the A.T. is marked by an official signboard erected by the Pennsylvania Department of Transportation.

Road approaches to the Trail are as follows:

0.0 mi.   at the west end of the Clarks Ferry Bridge over the Susquehanna River, along US 22-322, the Trail takes the first road to the left, crossing the Juniata River, and entering Duncannon. There is limited parking at the west end of the Susquehanna River bridge. Parking is available on the streets of Duncannon.

10.3 mi. from the Susquehanna River, where the Trail crosses PA 850 west of the Village of Keystone (approximately 9 miles west of US 11 & 15 at Marysville) there are two Game Commission parking areas. One is located 0.4 mi. north of the highway at the end of a gravel road. This parking area may be closed to the public at certain times of the year. The other is located 0.4 mi. east of the gravel road on the south side of PA 850. A new AT parking lot is located on the south side of Pa. Rt. 850, 0.2 mi. east of Miller's Gap Road.

14.6 mi. from the Susquehanna River where the trail crosses
PA 944, just east of Donnellytown. Extremely
limited parking can be found on Deer Lane. Do not
trespass. Exercise caution crossing PA 944.

SHELTERS AND DESIGNATED CAMPSITES

5.3 mi. from the Susquehanna River is the Thelma Marks
Memorial Shelter, built in 1960. An intermittent
spring is 400 ft. downhill on a blue-blazed trail.

12.6 mi. from the Susquehanna River is the Darlington
Shelter constructed in the spring of 1977, by the
Mountain Club of Maryland. The spring is
approximately 0.25 miles from the shelter.

PUBLIC ACCOMMODATIONS

Just beyond the west end of the Clarks Ferry Bridge in the
Village of Amity Hall, are motels and a restaurant.
Duncannon offers lodging, restaurants, a laundromat, a
pharmacy, and other places of business, which hikers will
find accommodating. Map immediately preceding this
section shows location of these services.

SUPPLIES

Supplies may be purchased in Duncannon at a number of
stores.

DUNCANNON

The Borough of Duncannon takes special pride in its claim
to be the approximate midpoint of the Appalachian Trail.
Consequently, a special community effort is made to
accommodate hikers. The Borough has posted a hiker
facility map at either end of town.

TRAIL DESCRIPTION

SECTION 9

SUSQUEHANNA RIVER TO PA 944

NORTH TO SOUTH

Miles   Detailed Trail Data

0.0   From the west end of the Clarks Ferry Bridge take the first road to the left, crossing over the Juniata River and then crossing under railroad tracks. Turn right for 1 block on PA Rt. 849 (Newport Road), then turn left onto High Street.

1.7   Turn left onto Cumberland Street, then right onto Market Street, crossing the Little Juniata Creek. Cross under US Routes 11 and 15 and then turn left on the old road passing several places of business.

2.1   Cross the Shermans Creek bridge and continue on paved road for 0.2 miles. Trail turns sharply to the right and up an embankment. Trail ascends steeply onto the flank of Cove Mountain and in 0.5 miles joins an old mountain road ascending the north side of the ridge.

3.1   Cross a rock slide. Trail becomes a footpath.

3.4   Reach Hawk Rock with fine views of the rivers, the town of Duncannon, and farmlands to the north.

Miles   Detailed Trail Data

5.3   Blue-blazed trail to the left leads 500 feet to the
       Thelma Marks Memorial **SHELTER**. Intermittent
       SPRING is 400 ft. farther down the mountain on a
       blue-blazed trail.

6.2   A blue-blazed trail to the right leads steeply down
       the mountain to the service road of the Duncannon
       Water Company.

7.8   Cross pipeline clearing on Cove Mountain with fine
       views. An unmarked trail on the right leads down
       the mountain to a Game Commission parking lot.

8.2   Begin descent of mountain.

8.9   Cross stream.

9.1   A.T. turns left onto woods road.

9.4   Trail turns right onto another woods road.

9.7   A.T. turns left through woods and field.

10.3   Reach PA Rt. 850; cross the road and continue
       across the farm field. A.T. parking lot is to the
       right.

10.5   Turn right at row of trees and follow Trail bearing
       diagonally to the left across the farm.

10.7   Cross Millers Gap Road and continue across the
       field.

10.8   Turn left into wooded ravine, passing remnants of
       an old farmstead.

11.2   Reach former telephone cable clearing. Trail turns
       left and ascends Little Mtn.

Miles   Detailed Trail Data

11.5   A.T. turns right.

11.7   After descending Little Mtn., trail turns right onto
        woods road.

12.3   A.T. turns left and begins ascent of Blue Mtn.

12.6   Blue-blazed trail on left leads to the Darlington
        SHELTER in approx. 200 yds. and **SPRING**. in
        approx. 0.25 mile from the shelter.

12.7   Cross ridgetop jeep road. Orange blazes mark the
        Darlington Trail on the left which follows the jeep
        road.   The blue blazed Tuscorora Trail is on the
        right.

13.0   Pass rock outcrop off the trail to the right which
        provides a good overlook across the Cumberland
        Valley. Trail continues to descend via switchbacks
        and an old road.

13.3   Turn right onto woods road. Seasonal **SPRING** to
        the right just beyond the turn.

13.4   Turn left off woods road and continues
        descending.

13.6   Trail crosses old dirt road. Piped **SPRING** 50 ft. to
        the right.

14.6   Reach PA 944, just east of Donnellytown, and the
        end of this section. The Trail crosses the highway
        and continues straight ahead. Exercise caution
        when crossing PA 944. The highway crossing is
        dangerous due to high speeds and limited sight
        distance - cross quickly.

SECTION 9

PA 944 TO SUSQUEHANNA RIVER

SOUTH TO NORTH

<u>Miles</u>   <u>Detailed Trail Data</u>

0.0   From PA 944, just east of Donnellytown, the Trail proceeds toward Blue Mountain.

1.0   Trail crosses dirt road. Piped **SPRING** 50 ft to the right. Enter partially timbered area and begin ascent of Blue Mountain.

1.2   Turn right onto woods road.

1.3   Reach seasonal **SPRING**. Just past the spring turn left, leaving woods road and resume ascent.

1.6   Pass rock outcrop off the trail to the left which provides a good overlook across the Cumberland Valley.

1.9   Cross ridgetop jeep road. Orange blazes mark the Darlington Trail on the right which follows the jeep road.   The blue blazed Tuscorora Trail is on the left.

2.0   Blue-blazed trail on right leads to the Darlington **SHELTER** in approx. 200 yds. and to a **SPRING** in approx. 0.25 mile from the shelter A.T. begins descent of Blue Mountain.

2.3   A.T. turns right onto woods road.

<u>Miles</u>   <u>Detailed Trail Data</u>

2.9   A.T. turns left and ascends Little Mtn.

3.1   Reach telephone cable clearing. A.T. turns left and
       follows clearing. Trail turns right into the woods.

3.4   Reach end of wooded ravine passing remnants of
       an old farmstead.

3.9   Reach Millers Gap Road; cross the road and
       continue diagonally across the field to the left.

4.1   Trail turns left through row of trees and continues
       across farm field.

4.3   Reach PA Rt. 850 with A.T. parking lot on left.
       Cross the road into farm field with blazed posts.

4.6   Enter woods.

4.9   Turn right onto woods road.

5.2   Trail turns left onto woods road.

5.5   A.T. turns right onto a woods road.

5.7   Cross stream and soon begin ascent of Cove Mtn.

6.8   Unmarked trail on leads down the mountain to a
       Game Commission parking lot. Cross pipeline
       clearing on Cove Mountain with fine views.

8.4   A blue-blazed trail to the left leads steeply down to
       the service road of the Duncannon Water
       Company.

9.3   Blue-blazed trail to the right leads 500 ft. to the
       Thelma Marks Memorial **SHELTER**. Intermittent
       SPRING is 400 ft. further down the mountain on a
       blue-blazed trail.

Miles   Detailed Trail Data

11.2   Reach Hawk Rock with good views of the rivers,
the town of Duncannon, and farmlands to the
north. Begin descent of north side of Cove Mtn.

11.5   Cross a rock slide. Trail becomes an old road.

11.9   Old road becomes a trail which crosses the nose of
Cove Mtn. and descends to the old highway across
the road from the old motel and bar. Turn sharp
left following the highway for 0.2 miles to
Shermans Creek bridge.

12.5   Cross bridge over Shermans Creek and continue
straight ahead on the old highway passing several
places of business.

12.8   Reach the junction of PA 274. Trail turns right
passing under US Rts. 11 & 15 and continues
ahead crossing the Little Juniata Creek and
entering the center of Duncannon on Market
Street. Trail then turns left onto Cumberland
Street and right onto High Street. See special note
regarding the Borough of Duncannon at the
introduction to this section.

14.1   Turn right onto PA Rt. 849 (Newport Road).

14.2   Turn left crossing under a railroad overpass and
then crossing the bridge over the Juniata River.

14.6   Reach the west end of the Clarks Ferry Bridge over
the Susquehanna River. This is the end of this
section. To continue on A.T. cross the bridge.

SECTION 10

PA 944 TO BOILING SPRINGS

DISTANCE: 12.3 Miles

This section of the Trail is maintained by the Cumberland Valley Appalachian Trail Management Association.

OVERVIEW OF SECTION 10

From PA 944 the Trail goes south through woods, then reaches and follows the Conodoguinet Creek for approximately 1.5 miles. After leaving the creek, the trail traverses a mixture of woods, farm pastures and cultivated fields on its way to Boiling Springs. Pastures and cultivated fields provide little shade, and summer hiking can be hot and dry. CARRY WATER.

GENERAL INFORMATION

MAPS

Use KTA Sections 9 & 10 black and white map or color Map #1, "Cumberland Valley," published by the Potomac Appalachian Trail Club.

ROAD APPROACHES

At some highways the A.T. is marked by an official signboard erected by the Pennsylvania Department of Transportation.

Road approaches to the trail are as follows:

This section of the Trail is unusual in that the trail crosses a dozen hard-surfaced public roads in the course of traversing the highly developed Cumberland Valley. Parking is available at many places, in addition to the following designated sites (distances from Pa. Route 944):

0.9 mi. Parking along the east side of Sherwood Drive.

2.0 mi. Limited parking at the Scott Farm Trail Work Center. Register with resident caretaker prior to leaving vehicle.

3.6 mi. Where the A.T. leaves Bernhisel Road following a farm lane between a baseball field and a pasture fence. Limited parking is available on the north side of the ball field along the pasture fence. Please do not block the farm lane.

10.3 mi. Where the A.T. crosses Pa. Route 74 (York Road), parking is available on the north side of the road, adjacent to the west side of an old barn foundation.

12.3 mi. Limited parking is available at the Appalachian Trail Conference Regional Office. Please register with office staff. Additional parking available at township historical park, Pa. Fish Commission parking area, and along village streets.

SHELTERS AND DESIGNATED CAMPSITES

There are no shelters in this section.

There is no camping or campfires permitted in this section.

PUBLIC ACCOMMODATIONS

1.2 mi.   east of the Trail on US 11, in the village of New
          Kingstown, is a motel and deli.

0.5 mi.   west of the Trail on US 11 are several motels and
          restaurants near the Interstate 81 interchange.

SUPPLIES

Located in Boiling Springs are a bank, post office,
restaurants and convenience stores.

Approximately 2.0 miles from Pa. 944, before crossing
Conodoguinet Creek, there is a store located in an old red
barn building at the west end of the trailer park near
Bernhisel Bridge, about 0.5 mi. from the Trail.

TRAIL DESCRIPTION

SECTION 10

PA 944 TO BOILING SPRINGS

NORTH TO SOUTH

Miles	Detailed Trail Data
0.0	From PA 944 just east of Donnellytown, the Trail leads south through woods
0.9	Reach paved Sherwood Drive and follow it for approximately 150 yards, before re-entering woods. For most of the next mile, the Trail follows alongside the Conodoguinet Creek.
2.0	Reach paved road across from the Scott Farm Trail Work Center, where potable water is available. The A.T. turns left, crossing the creek on pedestrian foot bridge attached to Bernhisel Bridge. After crossing creek, turn right and follow along the east bank of the creek.
3.0	Cross Bernhisel Road. Turn right and follow trail on a farm lane passing a fenced farm pasture.
3.4	Cross Interstate 81 on overpass and turn right off of Bernhisel Road.
4.3	Cross U.S. 11 on pedestrian bridge.
5.5	Cross Pa. Turnpike (I-76) on highway overpass.

Miles   Detailed Trail Data

5.8   Cross Appalachian Drive; enter woods and then pastures.

6.5   Cross Old Stonehouse Road.

7.1   Cross Ridge Road.

8.2   Cross Trindle Road.

8.6   Cross Byers Road.

9.2   Cross Lisburn Road. Trail mostly follows field hedgerows in this area.

10.3   Cross Pa. 74 (York Road). Trail traverses field, enters woods, and reaches high ground affording good views.

12.0   Reach Pa. 174 and turn right, following the road into Boiling Springs.

12.3   Reach Boiling Springs Village. Across from the Post Office, the trail turns left, leaving Pa. 174, and continuing south past the Appalachian Trail Conference Mid-Atlantic Regional Office. Potable water is available at ATC office.

SECTION 10

BOILING SPRINGS TO PA 944

SOUTH TO NORTH

<u>Miles</u>	<u>Detailed Trail Data</u>
0.0	From the Boiling Springs Post Office, the trail heads north by following Pa. Rt. 174 out of the town.
0.3	Trail turns left into field, leaving the highway. Begin passage through alternating farm fields and wooded areas and reaches high ground affording good views.
2.0	Cross Pa. Rt. 74 (York Road).
3.1	Cross Lisburn Road.
3.7	Cross Byers Road.
4.1	Cross Trindle Road.
5.2	Cross Ridge Road.
5.8	Cross Old Stonehouse Road; pass through pastures and then woods.
6.5	Cross Appalachian Drive.
6.8	Cross Pa. Turnpike (I-76) on highway overpass.
8.0	Cross U.S. Rt. 11 on pedestrian bridge.

Miles   Detailed Trail Data

8.9   Reach Bernhisel Road; turn left and follow
           alongside the road across the overpass above
           Interstate 81. Go 150 ft. Trail turns right off road
           and in short distance turns left and parallels road
           through farm field.

9.3   Cross Bernhisel Road, pass through pasture and
           fields, then follow along the east bank of
           Conodoguinet Creek.

10.3   Reach paved road and turn left, crossing the creek
           on pedestrian foot bridge attached to Bernhisel
           Bridge. At west end of bridge, on the left, is the
           Scott Farm Trail Work Center, where potable water
           can be obtained. Approximately 30 yards past the
           bridge, the A.T. turns right and for most of the
           next mile follows along the west bank of the
           Conodoguinet Creek.

11.4   Reach paved Sherwood Drive and follow it for
           approximately 150 yards, before re-entering
           woods.

12.3   Reach PA Rt. 944, just east of Donnellytown. Trail
           crosses road and continues north through woods.
           PA Rt. 944 is a dangerous road crossing. Exercise
           caution crossing PA Rt. 944.

SECTION 11

BOILING SPRINGS TO PA 94

DISTANCE: 8.8 Miles

This section of the Trail is maintained by the Cumberland Valley Appalachian Trail Management Association from Boiling Springs to Center Point Knob, and by the Mountain Club of Maryland from Center Point Knob to Route 94.

OVERVIEW OF SECTION 11

From Boiling Springs south, the Trail follows along the east shore of Children's Lake, then through farm fields for one mile before entering woods and beginning the climb to Center Point Knob. The last seven miles of the section is in the woods and has a series of climbs and descents with elevation changes of about 500 feet. Points of interest include the lake and springs in Boiling springs, the restored iron furnace and old mining sites, White Rocks Ridge via a side trail, and Rocky Ridge where the Trail passes through a maze of rock formations.

GENERAL INFORMATION

MAPS

Use KTA Sections 11 & 12 black and white map or color Map #1, "Cumberland Valley," published by the Potomac Appalachian Trail Club.

ROAD APPROACHES

At some highways the A.T. is marked by an official signboard erected by the Pennsylvania Department of Transportation.

Road approaches to the Trail are as follows:

0.0 mi. in Boiling Springs there is limited parking at the Appalachian Trail Conference regional office. (Please register with office staff.) Additional parking is available at the township historical park, the Pennsylvania Fish Commission parking area, and along village streets.

South of Churchtown there is limited parking along Kuhn Road, 0.7 mi. from the junction with Creek Road, with access to the A.T. via the White Rocks Ridge side trail (1.3 mi. to the A.T.).

6.0 mi. from Boiling Springs, where the Trail crosses Whiskey Spring Road, there is limited parking along the side of the road.

8.6 mi. from Boiling Springs, where the Trail crosses Sheet Iron Road, there is parking along the side of the road.

8.8 mi. from Boiling Springs, where the Trail crosses PA 94, there is very limited parking. Do not trespass.

SHELTERS AND DESIGNATED CAMPSITES

3.9 mi. from Boiling Springs there is the Alec Kennedy Shelter.

PUBLIC ACCOMMODATIONS

Bed and breakfast inns and restaurants are located in the village of Boiling Springs.

There are motels and restaurants in the town of Mount Holly Springs, located 2.5 miles north of the A.T. on PA 94.

SUPPLIES

A bank, post office, restaurants, and convenience stores are located in Boiling Springs.

Supplies can also be purchased in the town of Mount Holly Springs.

TRAIL DESCRIPTION

SECTION 11

BOILING SPRINGS TO PA 94

NORTH TO SOUTH

Miles   Detailed Trail Data

0.0   Potable water available at ATC office. From PA
       Rt. 174, across from the Boiling Springs village
       Post Office, the Trail leads south past the
       Appalachian Trail Conference's Mid-Atlantic
       Regional Field Office, and then follows along the
       east shore of Children's Lake. Beyond the lake,
       cross the road into a township park with a restored
       iron furnace.

0.3   Cross Yellow Breeches Creek (a notable trout
       stream) on a stone arch highway bridge, cross very
       active railroad tracks, turning right into farm fields
       at gated entrance and follow blazed posts. The
       only designated campsite in the Cumberland Valley
       A.T. section is down a driveway on the left to an
       abandoned stone farmhouse next to the railroad
       tracks.

1.1   Cross Leidigh Road and follow blazed posts
       through a cultivated field.

1.7   Enter woods and begin gradual climb toward
       Center Point Knob. Pass evidence of old mine
       operations.

<u>Miles</u>   <u>Detailed Trail Data</u>

3.0   Reach Center Point Knob, the one-time mid-point
       of the A.T. Begin descent from summit and,
       within 100 yards, reach blue-blazed side trail
       leading left which is the White Rocks Ridge Trail.
       The White Rocks Ridge Trail (former A.T.) follows
       the ridge, winding through and over outcroppings
       of hard quartzite rock, dating back some 550
       million years. White Rocks forms one of the
       outlines of the greater South Mountain and marks
       the northern terminus of the Blue Ridge Mountains.
       The trail is rough and rocky, and slippery in wet
       weather.
       The White Rocks Ridge Trail leads 1.3 miles to
       Kuhn Road.

3.9   A blue-blazed trail leads left to the Alec Kennedy
       SHELTER, 850 feet from the A.T.

4.0   Cross a woods road with orange blazes, which to
       the left leads 1.7 miles to Boy Scout Camp
       Tuckahoe. Immediately cross Little Dogwood Run
       and pass through an old charcoal hearth.

4.8   Cross a pipeline that looks like a narrow road, then
       ascend Little Rocky Ridge through the woods.

5.5   Pass a rock outcrop on the left with a view and
       descend down ridge.

6.0   Turn left onto Whiskey Spring Road. On the left in
       30 yds pass Whiskey **SPRING** which is always
       flowing. Turn right uphill following the crest of
       Rocky Ridge through a maze of rock formations,
       with a good view of Cumberland Valley to the
       right.

7.0   Pass vista on the right. A.T. descends Rocky
       Ridge by switchbacks.

Miles   Detailed Trail Data

7.4   Cross Old Town Road (dirt road).

7.5   Cross old road.

7.8   Cross old road, then telephone line right-of-way,
         then stream.

7.9   Trail bears right at junction.

8.1   Cross stream.

8.6   Cross Sheet Iron Road. Blue-blazed side trail leads
         0.3 mi. to Moyers Campground. Store where
         showers are available.

8.7   Cross under a power line.

8.8   Reach PA 94 at a point 2.5 mi. south of Mount
         Holly Springs.

         To continue on A.T. cross highway.

SECTION 11

PA 94 TO BOILING SPRINGS

SOUTH TO NORTH

<u>Miles</u>	<u>Detailed Trail Data</u>

0.0   From PA 94, the Trail enters the woods at a point 2.5 mi. South of Mount Holly Springs.

0.1   Cross under a power line.

0.2   Cross Sheet Iron Road. Blue-blazed side trail leads 0.3 mi. to Moyers Campground. Store where showers are available.

0.7   Cross stream.

1.0   Cross stream, then telephone line right-of-way, then old road.

1.3   Cross old road.

1.4   Cross Old Town Road (dirt road) and ascend Rocky Ridge by switchbacks.

1.8   Reach top of ridge and view of Cumberland Valley. A.T. now follows the ridge crest passing through a maze of rock formations to the east end of the ridge, then descends to Whiskey Spring Road.

2.8   Turn left onto Whiskey Spring Road. In 30 yds. pass Whiskey **SPRING** on the right, always flowing. Turn right into the woods. Ascend Little Rocky Ridge.

Miles   Detailed Trail Data

3.3   Pass a rock outcrop on the right with a view and descend ridge through the woods.

4.0   Cross a pipeline that looks like a narrow road. Ascend Murphy Hill (Cabin Hill) and descend to a charcoal hearth.

4.8   Cross Little Dogwood Run. Immediately cross a trail blazed with orange markings which to the right leads in 1.7 mi. to Boy Scout Camp Tuckahoe. Ascend and descend the side of Colon Hill; 300 feet after crossing Little Dogwood Run.

4.9   A blue-blazed trail leads right to the Alec Kennedy **SHELTER**, 850 feet from the A.T. Continue ascent and then descend from the side of Colon Hill.

5.8   Blue-blazed side trail leads right to the White Rocks Ridge Trail. The A.T., bearing left, ascends 100 yards to Center Point Knob, the one-time mid-point of the A.T. The White Rocks Ridge Trail (former A.T.) follows the ridge, winding through and over outcroppings of hard quartzite rock before descending and reaching Kuhn Road in 1.3 miles. The ancient quartzite rock, dating back some 550 million years, forms one of the outlines of the greater South Mountain and marks the northern terminus of the Blue Ridge Mountains. The trail is rough and rocky, and slippery in wet weather.

6.8   Pass evidence of old mine operations.

7.1   Enter farm field and follow blazed posts.

<u>Miles</u>   <u>Detailed Trail Data</u>

7.7   Cross Leidigh Road.

8.5   Cross Yellow Breeches Creek on a stone arch
        highway bridge. Pass a township park with a
        restored iron furnace, and then follow along the
        east shore of Children's Lake.

8.8   Reach PA Rt. 174, across from the Boiling Springs
        village Post Office and adjacent to the Appalachian
        Trail Conference's Mid-Atlantic Regional Field
        Office. To continue north, turn right and follow PA
        Rt. 174. Potable water available at ATC office.

SECTION 12

PA 94 TO PINE GROVE FURNACE

DISTANCE: 10.9 Miles

This section of the Trail is maintained by the Mountain Club of Maryland.

OVERVIEW OF SECTION 12

This section is generally in the woods for the entire route. After leaving PA 94, climb and descend Trents Hill, then ascend Piney Mountain, walking along the ridge before descending to Pine Grove Furnace State Park. Points of interest are the sheer, conspicuous quartzite cliffs and splendid view of the lakes at Pole Steeple, 0.5 mile off the Trail atop Piney Mountain; and the ruins of the old Pine Grove Furnace. The park office houses a small, but interesting, museum of the natural and industrial history of the area.

GENERAL INFORMATION

MAPS

Use KTA Sections 11 & 12 black and white map or color Map #2-3 (combined), "Michaux State Forest, Pennsylvania," published by the Potomac Appalachian Trail Club.

ROAD APPROACHES

At some highways the A.T. is marked by an official signboard erected by the Pennsylvania Department of Transportation.

Road approaches to the Trail are as follows:

0.0 mi. at PA 94, the Trail crosses 2.5 miles south of Mount Holly Springs. Limited parking.

0.3 mi. from PA 94, parking is available where the A.T. crosses Sheet Iron Road.

2.0 mi. from PA 94, the Trail crosses PA 34. Limited parking.

2.8 mi. from PA 94, the Trail crosses Hunters Run Road. Limited parking.

10.6 mi. from PA 94, in Pine Grove Furnace State Park there is adequate parking. Check at the Park office for regulations governing the parking of vehicles.

HUNTERS RUN ROAD

The road referred to in this section as "Hunters Run Road" is shown on some maps as Pine Grove Road, and an occasional sign to that effect may still be encountered.

SHELTERS AND DESIGNATED CAMPSITES

3.3 mi. from PA 94 is a blue-blazed trail leading 0.2 miles to the Tagg Run Shelter with a raised sleeping platform. A spring is 100 feet beyond the shelters. An unusual outhouse facility is at the site.

PUBLIC ACCOMMODATIONS

There are motels and restaurants in Mount Holly Springs, 2.5 miles north of the Trail from both PA 94 and PA 34. Pine Grove Furnace State Park offers campsites and swimming facilities. There is also a seasonal snack bar in the Park. The Ironmasters Mansion Hostel of American Youth Hostels is also in the park at Route 233 and the A.T.

SUPPLIES

Supplies may be purchased in Mount Holly Springs. In Pine Grove Furnace State Park there is a small store 50 yards off the Trail on the south side of PA 233. The store is seasonal and is generally open seven days a week between Memorial Day and Labor Day, although it may be open at other times. West of the Pine Grove Road crossing along Pine Grove Road are two public campgrounds. Tagg Run Campground (0.4 miles) has a small camp store and snack bar which is open year round. Mountain Creek Campground (1.4 miles) has a camp store.

TRAIL DESCRIPTION

SECTION 12

PA 94 TO PINE GROVE FURNACE

NORTH TO SOUTH

<u>Miles</u>   <u>Detailed Trail Data</u>

0.0   Enter the woods at a point 2.5 mi. south of Mount
Holly Springs on PA 94 ascending to a woods road
on Trents Hill.

0.2   Turn left on woods road. A stand of mountain
laurel bushes to the right of the footpath are
covered with blossoms in the springtime.

0.4   The trail turns to the left, leaving the woods road
and winding through the woods. There are many
sassafras trees and blueberry bushes in this
section.

1.1   Turn right onto a broader trail, a portion of which
may have been a woods road. Turn left and
descend Trents Hill.

1.8   Reach PA 34, turn left, cross stream on highway
bridge, and bear right into a field. Cross the
railroad track and bear left along old rail bed.

Miles   Detailed Trail Data

2.9   Cross Hunters Run Road.

3.2   Cross Tagg Run. A blue-blazed trail to the left
        leads 0.2 mi. to the Tagg Run **SHELTER** with a
        SPRING 100 feet beyond. Do not drink water from
        Tagg Run; cows pasturing upstream cause
        contamination.

3.5   Trail bears left uphill.

4.6   Blue-blazed trail to the right leads downhill 0.7 mi.
        to Hunters Run Road and Mountain Creek
        Campground.

4.9   Cross Limekiln Road. To the left, it leads to the
        Village of Goodyear. To the right, it leads 0.9 mi.
        downhill to Hunters Run Road.

5.9   Turn left at a junction with a blue-blazed trail (not
        maintained) which comes up from Hunters Run
        Road.

8.0   Cross Old Forge Road and begin descending Piney
        Mountain on a forest service road. Blue-blazed trail
        to the right leads 0.5 mi. to Pole Steeple, a cliff
        with a great view. From there, a blue-blazed trail
        descends the cliff face and in 0.6 mi. reaches an
        abandoned railroad bed that is now a road in the
        state park.

9.5   Turn left onto the old railroad bed, now a park
        road, leading to Fuller Lake.

10.1   Cross foot bridge with beach ahead and
        immediately turn right and cross another foot
        bridge.

<u>Miles</u>   <u>Detailed Trail Data</u>

10.5   Reach a locked gate. Continuing through the park,
        note the ruins of the old Pine Grove Furnace on
        your right.

10.6   Turn right on paved road and in 50 yds turn left
        passing Ironmasters Mansion American Youth
        Hostel on right. At the left turn is a seasonal
        grocery store in the white building on the right.

10.8   Turn left onto PA Rt. 233.

10.9   Cross PA 233 onto a gravel road.

SECTION 12

PINE GROVE FURNACE TO PA 94

SOUTH TO NORTH

<u>Miles</u>   <u>Detailed Trail Data</u>

0.0   At the intersection of a gravel road with PA 233
         turn left along the highway for 200 yards and then
         bear right onto Bendersville Road. Pass the
         Ironmasters Mansion American Youth Hostel on
         your left.

0.2   Cross a paved road and then bear left on a park
         road. A seasonal grocery store is 50 yards to your
         left on the paved road in an old white building.
         The Trail continues ahead through the picnic
         grounds. Note the ruins of the old Pine Grove
         Furnace on the left.

0.4   Continue past a locked gate on an old railroad bed,
         now a park road, passing Fuller Lake on the right.

0.8   Cross foot bridge and immediately turn left and
         cross another foot bridge.

1.4   Turn right ascending an old mountain road known
         as Petersburg Road.

Miles   Detailed Trail Data

2.9   Reach the top of Piney Mountain and cross Old
         Forge Road. A blue-blazed trail to the left leads
         0.5 mi. to Pole Steeple, a cliff with a great view.
         From there a blue-blazed trail descends the cliff
         face and in 0.6 mi. reaches an abandoned railroad
         bed, now a park road.

3.2   Turn left into the woods.

5.0   Turn right uphill where a blue-blazed trail (not
         maintained) comes in from the left.

6.0   Cross Limekiln Road. To the right it leads to the
         Village of Goodyear. To the left it leads 0.9 mi.
         downhill to Hunters Run Road.

6.3   Blue-blazed trail to the left leads downhill 0.7 mi.
         to Hunters Run Road and Mountain Creek
         Campground.

7.4   Trail turns right.

7.7   Blue-blazed trail to the right leads 0.2 mi. to the
         Tagg Run **SHELTER** with a **SPRING** 100 feet
         beyond. A.T. continues ahead, crossing Tagg Run.
         Do not drink water from Tagg Run; cows pasturing
         upstream cause contamination.

8.0   Cross Hunters Run Road. Turn right onto old rail
         bed.

9.0   Turn right, crossing tracks and crossing old field.

Miles   Detailed Trail Data

9.1   Reach PA 34. A.T. turns left, crosses stream on highway bridge, and turns right.

9.2   Begin ascent of Trents Hill.

9.8   Bear left onto a footpath which winds through areas thick with sassafras trees and blueberry bushes

10.5   Turn right onto a woods road where mountain laurel blooms to the left of the trail in the springtime.

10.7   Turn right descending to PA 94.

10.9   Reach PA 94. To the left, in 2.5 mi. is the Village of Mount Holly Springs. A.T. continues across highway and into the woods.

SECTION 13

PINE GROVE FURNACE TO CALEDONIA

DISTANCE: 19.7 Miles

This section of the Trail is maintained by individual overseers and the North Chapter of the Potomac Appalachian Trail Club.

OVERVIEW OF SECTION 13

Leaving Pine Grove Furnace State Park the first six miles is a gradual ascent to the plateau-like top of South Mountain, then along the plateau with minor changes in elevation to a rather steep descent to Caledonia State Park. Points of interest along the Trail are the preserved ruins of the old iron furnace in Pine Grove Furnace State Park and the small but interesting museum depicting the natural and industrial history of the area. See the Chapter on History. Going south, the Trail passes the site of the former Pine Grove Furnace Cabin of the PATC, once a farmhouse. One passes many circular flat charcoal burning hearths, 30 to 50 feet in diameter.

In the former Camp Michaux property, the trail passes the one remaining wall of a huge stone barn dating from the early days. For several years Keystone Trails Association held its fall meeting at this church camp. In World War II it had been a prisoner-of-war camp for captured German submarine personnel, and before that, a CCC Camp. The trail shelters and the Milesburn Cabin were built by the CCC about 1935.

A model iron furnace and the Thaddeus Stevens Museum are along US 30 in Caledonia State Park, 0.6 miles east of the trail.

This section is located mainly in Michaux State Forest. Therefore, all rules and regulations must be followed.

GENERAL INFORMATION

MAPS

Use KTA Sections 13 & 14 black and white map or color Map #2-3 (combined), "Michaux State Forest, Pennsylvania," published by the Potomac Appalachian Trail Club.

ROAD APPROACHES

PATC North Chapter has erected AT signs at roadways.

Road approaches to the Trail are as follows:

0.0 mi. in Pine Grove Furnace State Park, there is adequate parking. Contact the Park Office for regulations governing the extended parking of vehicles.

2.0 mi. from Pine Grove Furnace State Park, the Trail crosses Michaux Road, also called High Mountain Road, at the site of the former Camp Michaux. Limited parking. No protection from vandalism.

8.4 mi. from Pine Grove Furnace State Park, the Trail crosses the Arendtsville-Shippensburg Road. Parking. No protection from vandalism.

19.7 mi. from Pine Grove Furnace State Park, in Caledonia State Park, there is adequate parking. Contact the Park Office for location and for regulations governing the extended parking of vehicles.

Special Note: The Trail crosses many unimproved roads in this section, most of which are maintenance roads of the Michaux State Forest. Limited parking is possible at many of these crossings, but vandalism is an occasional problem.

SHELTERS AND DESIGNATED CAMPSITES

3.4 mi. from Pine Grove Furnace State Park are the twin Toms Run Shelters.

6.5 mi. from Pine Grove Furnace State Park is the Anna Michener Memorial Cabin of the PATC. This is a locked cabin with the capacity of 14 persons. Reservations to rent must be obtained in advance from the Potomac Appalachian Trail Club, 118 Park Street, SE, Vienna, VA 22180; telephone 703/242-0693 weekday evenings.

9.6 mi. from Pine Grove Furnace State Park are the twin Birch Run Shelters.

12.1 mi.from Pine Grove Furnace State Park is the Milesburn Cabin of the PATC. This is a locked cabin with a capacity of 12 persons. Reservations to rent must be obtained in advance from PATC.

17.1 mi.from Pine Grove Furnace State Park are the twin Quarry Gap Shelters.

PUBLIC ACCOMMODATIONS

There is a seasonal snack bar at Fuller Lake in Pine Grove Furnace State Park and a seasonal snack bar at the swimming pool in Caledonia State Park. East of Caledonia State Park, along US 30, is a restaurant within a mile; and in 2.1 miles, Colonel's Creek Campground where cabins can be rented. To the west on US 30, 2.5 miles, is the Rite Spot Motel and Restaurant. The Ironmasters Mansion Hostel (AYH) is open year round in Pine Grove Furnace State Park.

SUPPLIES

There is a small seasonal store in Pine Grove Furnace State Park, just off the trail near the Park headquarters. There is a grocery store 0.9 miles west of the trail along US 30.

TRAIL DESCRIPTION

SECTION 13

PINE GROVE FURNACE TO CALEDONIA

NORTH TO SOUTH

<u>Miles</u>	<u>Detailed Trail Data</u>

0.0   The Trail leaves PA 233 about 200 yards west of the park headquarters on a gravel road to the north.

0.1   Where the gravel road ends, bear right and in 40 yds bear left onto an old woods road.

0.7   Leaving the woods road pass several charcoal flats which provided fuel for Pine Grove Furnace in the 1700's.

1.3   Blue-blazed Sunset Rocks Trail leads to the left. (For detailed trail data see the end of this section.) Parking lot is at end of old Shippensburg Road 50 yds on right. Continuing straight ahead in 30 yds cross Toms Run in foot bridge and turn left onto Old Shippensburg Road.

1.6   Short trail to the left leads 50 yards to Halfway **SPRING**.

Miles   Detailed Trail Data

2.0   Reach a clearing, the site of the former Camp
           Michaux, and the ruins of a large stone barn. A.T.
           turns right onto Michaux Road, also called High
           Mountain Road. To the left, off Michaux Road, is
           a carved rock plaque noting that Camp Michaux
           was the site of a World War II prisoner of war
           camp.

2.2   Trail turns left onto an abandoned road.

3.4   Reach the twin Toms Run **SHELTERS**. **SPRING** is
           behind the shelters.

3.5   After crossing Toms Run the blue-blazed Sunset
           Rocks Trail comes in from the left. A.T. now
           ascends the steep slope of Antmire Hill.

4.6   Cross Woodrow Road, a forestry road passable by
           auto.

5.2   At the boundary of the private Tumbling Run Game
           Preserve turn right, paralleling Ridge Road which is
           a short distance to the right. (CAUTION: Do not
           follow the Michaux Forest boundary markers,
           which are also white paint.) No camping or fires in
           the preserve.

5.9   Cross the entrance road to the Preserve and
           immediately leave Preserve land.

6.5   Blue-blazed trail to the left leads east 0.2 mi. to
           the locked Anna Michener Memorial Cabin of the
           PATC. (See "Shelters" in General Information.)
           A.T. now follows cabin entrance road to right.

7.2   Approximately 40 yds before gate bear left into
           woods.

Miles   Detailed Trail Data

7.3   Cross the old bed of Dead Woman Hollow Road,
        now a winter snowmobile trail.

8.3   Cross the Arendtsville-Shippensburg Road.
        Limited parking is available.

9.7   Cross Birch Run and arrive at the twin Birch Run
        SHELTERS. **SPRING** is to your right.

10.3   Cross the old bed of Fegley Hollow Road and under
        a powerline.

11.0   Cross Michaux Forest's Rocky Knob Trail, a loop
        nature trail to the left. Ridge Road is a short
        distance to the right.

11.7   Cross Ridge Road and descend steeply.

12.1   Cross Milesburn Road. Ahead is the locked
        Milesburn Cabin of the PATC. (See Shelters in
        General Information.) A blue-blazed trail to the
        right leads downstream and across Milesburn road
        to a **SPRING**. From the Milesburn Cabin climb
        steeply.

12.5   Cross the intersection of Canada Hollow Road,
        Means Hollow Road, and Ridge Road.

12.9   Cross Dughill Trail.

13.0   Cross Middle Ridge Road. Turn right and go 70
        yds. Cross road and reenter woods. The A.T. now
        parallels Ridge Road for the next 1.4 miles.

14.4   Cross old woods road.

14.8   Cross a power line cut.

Miles   Detailed Trail Data

15.6   Reach the junction of Ridge Road and Stillhouse
        Road in an area known as Sandy Sod. A.T. goes
        ahead on Ridge Road for 0.1 miles then turns left
        into the woods and descends through Quarry Gap.

16.3   Hosack Run Trail takes off to the left joining the
        Locust Gap Trail in 1.1 miles. (In combination with
        the A.T., this provides a beautiful circuit hike).

16.8   A.T. crosses a stream and turns left down stream
        valley.

17.0   Arrive at the twin Quarry Gap **SHELTERS**. Spring
        is located 10 yds north of shelter.

17.4   Pass a **SPRING** on the right and the site of the
        former Locked Antlers Camp on the left. The A.T.
        is gated here to control vehicle access to the
        Quarry Gap Shelters.

17.7   Turn right off Quarry Gap Road onto Greenwood
        Furnace Road. To your left, Locust Gap Trail leads
        1.8 miles to the Milesburn Road and to your right
        3.0 miles to Houser Road and to Fayetteville near
        US 30.

17.8   The A.T. turns left, then steeply descends
        Chinquapin Hill.

17.9   Where the Locust Gap Trail continues ahead, the
        A.T. turns left, passing the blue-blazed Caledonia
        Park Three Valley Trail. Pass two parking lots,
        with year-round rest rooms adjoining the second
        one. The road goes to the park office.

18.5   Bear left where a blue-blazed trail continues
        straight ahead.

<u>Miles</u>   <u>Detailed Trail Data</u>

18.9   Cross a wide park maintenance road. Pass two
       parking lots and seasonal restrooms.

19.3   Cross Conococheague Creek on Caledonia Park
       bridge.   A.T. bears to the right.

19.5   Cross bridge over former canal.

19.6   Turn left on footbridge over former canal.

19.7   Reach US. Rt. 30. PA 233 and Caledonia State
       Park parking lot are 0.6 mi. to the east. The
       Michaux District Forest office is an additional 0.8
       miles to the left.

DETAILED TRAIL DATA

SUNSET ROCKS TRAIL

PINE GROVE FURNACE CABIN SITE TO TOMS RUN SHELTERS

<u>Miles</u>	<u>Detailed Trail Data</u>
0.0	Where the A.T. first crosses Toms Run, the blue-blazed Sunset Rocks Trail keeps to the left of the run following a former woods road, and ascending.
0.2	Road becomes a trail ascending more steeply.
0.4	Reach the crest of Little Rocky Ridge, turn right (to the left, a short spur trail provides good views) and follow through and up over boulders. Use care!
1.1	Turn right onto Michaux (High Mountain) Road.
1.4	Turn left onto an old woods road, then follow the wire fence of the former Camp Michaux.
2.4	Reach the A.T., at 3.4 miles from PA 233 in Pine Grove Furnace Park, just 30 yards beyond its second crossing of Toms Run. Shelters are another 30 yards to the right.

DETAILED TRAIL DATA

SUNSET ROCKS TRAIL

TOMS RUN SHELTERS TO PINE GROVE FURNACE CABIN SITE

<u>Miles</u>　　<u>Detailed Trail Data</u>

0.0　　30 yards before reaching Toms Run and 60 yards before the shelters, this blue-blazed trail leads right, then along a wire fence of the former Camp Michaux for 0.5 mile.

1.0　　Turn right onto Michaux (High Mountain) Road.

1.3　　Turn left onto a woods road ascending Little Rocky Ridge.

1.9　　Reach the crest of Sunset Rocks and follow through up and over boulders. Use care!

2.0　　Turn left from the ridge crest and descend. A short spur trail goes straight ahead, providing good views.

2.4　　Reach the A.T. To the left, across Toms Run, is the site of the former Pine Grove Furnace Cabin of the PATC.

SECTION 13

CALEDONIA TO PINE GROVE FURNACE

SOUTH TO NORTH

__Miles__   __Detailed Trail Data__

0.0   Cross US Rt. 30. PA Rt. 233 and Caledonia State Park parking lot are 0.6 mi. to the east. The Michaux District Forest office is an additional 0.8 miles to the right.

0.2   Cross bridge over former canal.

0.4   Reach bridge over Conococheague Creek in Caledonia State Park. Pass two parking lots with year-round rest rooms beside the first one. Climb steeply between Orebank Hill on the left and Chinquapin Hill on the right.

0.8   Cross a wide park maintenance road. Pass two parking lots and seasonal restrooms.

1.8   The blue-blazed Caledonia Park Three Valley Trail comes in from the left.

2.0   Blue-blazed Locust Gap Trail comes in from the left 3.0 miles from the Fayetteville area on Greenwood Furnace Road near US Rt. 30 and leads 1.8 miles to the right to Milesburn Road.

2.3   Pass the site of the former Locked Antlers Camp and **SPRING** on the right. The A.T. is gated here to control vehicle access to the Quarry Gap Shelters.

Miles   Detailed Trail Data

2.7   Arrive at twin Quarry Gap **SHELTERS.** Spring is
       located 10 yds north of shelters.

2.9   A.T. crosses a stream.

3.4   Hosack Run Trail takes off to the right joining the
       Locust Gap Trail in 1.1 miles. (In combination with
       the A.T., this provides a beautiful circuit hike).

4.0   Reach the top of the hill and turn right onto Ridge
       Road.

4.1   Reach the junction of Stillhouse Road and Ridge
       Road in an area known as Sandy Sod.   Cross the
       intersection and turn left off Ridge Road into the
       woods.

4.9   Cross a powerline cut.

5.3   Cross an old woods road.

6.7   Cross Middle Ridge Road.

6.8   Cross Dughill Trail.

7.2   Cross the intersection of Canada Hollow Road,
       Means Hollow Road, and Ridge Road.

7.6   Reach the locked Milesburn Cabin of the PATC.
       Reservations to rent must be obtained in advance
       from PATC. (See Shelters in General Information)
       A blue-blazed trail to the left leads downstream
       and across Milesburn Road to a **SPRING**. A.T.
       crosses Milesburn Road and ascends steeply.

8.0   Cross Ridge Road. Pass under power line.

Miles   Detailed Trail Data

8.7   Cross Michaux Forest's Rocky Knob Trail, a loop
         nature trail. Ridge Road is a short distance to the
         left.

9.4   Cross under a power line and then cross the bed of
         former Fegley Hollow Road.

10.0   Arrive at twin Birch Run **SHELTERS** on the right.
         SPRING on your left. Trail continues ahead,
         crossing Birch Run.

11.4   Cross the Arendtsville-Shippensburg Road. Limited
         parking is available.

12.4   Cross the bed of the former Dead Woman Hollow
         Road, now a wintertime snowmobile trail. A long
         descent is ahead with views of Mount Holly and
         Long Mountain in the distance.

13.2   Blue-blazed trail to the right leads east 0.2 mile to
         the locked Anna Michener Memorial Cabin of the
         PATC. Reservations to rent must be obtained from
         the PATC in advance.

13.8   Cross the entrance road to the private Tumbling
         Run Game Preserve. No camping or fires in the
         preserve. Trail turns right, then left, generally
         following the boundary of the game preserve.

15.1   Cross Woodrow Road with fine views.

16.2   Blue-blazed Sunset Rocks Trail goes off to the
         right. For details of this trail, see the end of the
         North to South trail description for this section.

16.3   Arrive at the twin Toms Run **SHELTERS**.   **SPRING**
         in behind shelters.

Miles   Detailed Trail Data

17.4   Turn right onto Michaux Road, also called High
        Mountain Road, then passing into the site of the
        former Camp Michaux. A hand-carved, stone
        plaque noting that Camp Michaux was a World
        War II prisoner of war camp.

17.6   Trail turns left passing the ruins of an old stone
        barn.

18.1   A.T. bears right where the road forks. Side trail to
        the right leads 50 yards to Halfway **SPRING**.

18.4   Across the foot bridge the blue-blazed Sunset
        Rocks Trail leads uphill to the right. (For
        description see details at the end of the North to
        South trail). A.T. bears right crossing Toms Run
        on a foot bridge.

18.6   Cross a small brook, then pass old charcoal flats
        which provided fuel for Pine Grove Furnace in the
        1700's. Trail bears right, then left.

19.0   Trail follows an old woods road.

19.6   Turn right onto a gravel road.

19.7   Reach PA 233 and turn left for about 200 yards,
        then turn right onto Bendersville Road entering Pine
        Grove Furnace State Park. The first road to the
        left passes the seasonally operated park store, an
        old white building, in 50 yards, and continues on
        to the park headquarters building which is located
        on PA 233.

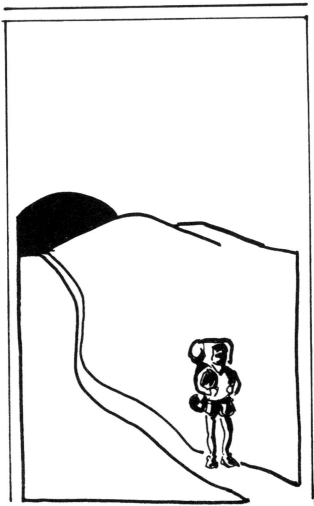

SECTION 14

CALEDONIA TO PEN MAR

DISTANCE: 17.9 Miles

This section of the Trail is maintained by individual overseers and the North Chapter of the Potomac Appalachian Trail Club.

OVERVIEW OF SECTION 14

Most of the Trail, in this section, is through pleasing woods on Rocky Mountain. The main climb to Snowy Mountain is gradual with a descent to the Old Forge Picnic Grounds area, and a steep climb up to Pen Mar. Watch out for the white paint boundary markings of Michaux State Forest Lands, which cross the A.T. and are similar to A.T. blazes, causing some confusion. The latter are 2" X 6" and face the hiker. The others are quite irregular. Points of interest along the trail are the Chimney Rocks and the Old Forge Picnic Ground. The Chapter on History details the story of Pen Mar Park and the Caledonia Park area.

This section is mainly located in Michaux State Forest. Therefore, all rules and regulations must be followed.

GENERAL INFORMATION

MAPS

Use KTA Section 14 Map or color Map #4, "Mont Alto Section" published by the Potomac Appalachian Trail Club.

ROAD APPROACHES

PATC North Chapter has erected AT signs at roadways.

Road approaches to the Trail are as follows:

0.0 mi.   on US Highway 30, at approximately the mid-point between Gettysburg and Chambersburg, the Trail crosses US 30 0.6 mi. west of the intersection with PA 233. Adequate parking nearby. Contact Caledonia State Park office for regulations governing the extended parking of vehicles.

4.6 mi.   from Caledonia State Park the Trail crosses PA 233. Limited parking. No protection from vandals. A "Vision Quest" project camp is 100 yards to the east.

9.8 mi.   from Caledonia State Park the Trail crosses Old Forge Road near the Old Forge Picnic Ground. Limited parking.

10.4 mi. from Caledonia State Park the Trail reaches the edge of the playing field of Old Forge Picnic Grounds. Parking for approximately 10 vehicles. Overnight parking must be cleared by Michaux State Forest office.

15.3 mi. from Caledonia State Park the Trail crosses PA 16 between Rouzerville and Blue Ridge Summit. Limited parking.

17.9 mi. from Caledonia State Park the Trail goes through
        the village of Pen Mar. Limited parking. Do not
        trespass. Parking is available in Pen Mar County
        Park in Maryland.

SHELTERS AND DESIGNATED CAMPSITES

3.0 mi. from Caledonia State Park are the Rocky Mountain
        Shelters on a side trail to the east. These have
        replaced the former Raccoon Run Shelters

8.3 mi. from Caledonia State Park is the locked Hermitage
        Cabin of the PATC, located 0.9 mile off the Trail.
        Reservations to rent must be obtained in advance
        from the Potomac Appalachian Trail Club, 118 Park
        Street, SE, Vienna, VA 22180; telephone
        703/242-0693 weekday evenings..

9.6 mi. from Caledonia State Park there are the two
        Tumbling Run Shelters along the trail.

10.8 mi. from Caledonia State Park is the Antietam Shelter
        just beyond the Old Forge Picnic Grounds.

13.2 mi. from Caledonia State Park are the two Deer Lick
        Shelters.

PUBLIC ACCOMMODATIONS

There is a seasonal snack bar at the swimming pool in
Caledonia State Park. East of Caledonia State Park, along
US 30, is a restaurant within a mile. To the east 2.1 miles,
Colonel's Creek Campground rents cabins. To the west on
US 30, 2.5 mi., is Rite Spot Motel and Restaurant. There is
one restaurant in Blue Ridge Summit, 1.8 mi. east of the
Trail on PA 16.

SUPPLIES

There is a grocery store 0.9 miles west of Caledonia State
Park along US 30. There is a pizza shop 0.5 mile west of
the park. In the village of South Mountain, about 5.0 miles
south of Caledonia State Park and 1.1 miles east of the
Trail, along Sanatorium Road, is located a grocery store and
gas station, as well as a post office. Along PA 16, there
are stores in Rouzerville 2.5 miles west of the Trail and in
Blue Ridge Summit 1.8 miles east of the trail.

TRAIL DESCRIPTION

SECTION 14

CALEDONIA TO PEN MAR

NORTH TO SOUTH

Miles   Detailed Trail Data

0.0   Cross US 30. To the left (east) 0.6 mi. is PA 233
          and Caledonia State Park parking lot. Michaux
          District Forester's office is 0.4 mi. beyond. To the
          right (west) 0.9 mi. are two stores, a motel, and
          restaurant in an additional 1.6 mi.

0.1   Cross gas pipe line clearing. Begin steady uphill
          climb.

1.4   A.T. follows top of ridge for next 1.6 mi.

3.0   Blue-blazed side trail to the east goes downhill
          0.15 mi. to the Rocky Mountain **SHELTERS**.   This
          trail continues another 0.26 mi. To PA Rt 223.
          The **SPRING** is another 0.1 mi. south on the west
          side of PA Rt 233.

3.2   A.T. descends off ridge to west side.

4.5   Cross a gravel maintenance road on ridge leading
          left 0.1 mi. to water tanks.

Miles   Detailed Trail Data

4.7   Reach PA Rt 233. To the left (east) 1.6 mi. is the village of South Mountain, with store and post office. PA 233 goes north to Caledonia State Park and US 30. To the right PA 233 goes to the village of Mont Alto, Mont Alto School of Forestry of Penn State University, and Mont Alto State Park. Vision Quest Camp entrance is visible to the left.

4.9   A.T. turns right as unmarked trail to left goes back to Caledonia State Park.

5.0   Turn left on Swamp Road through a very boggy area.

5.1   Turn right (south) off Swamp Road on a gravel road.

5.4   Cross dirt road (closed to public).

5.7   Cross Snowy Mountain Road. Ascend.

6.3   Cross under a power line.

7.5   Cross a pipeline.

8.3   Near summit of Buzzard Peak reach intersection with blue-blazed trail. A.T. continues ahead descending. The Blue-blazed trail to the left leads 120 yds to Chimney Rocks, at 1,940 feet of elevation, with a magnificent view over Green Ridge and the Waynesboro Reservoir. Blue-blazed trail to the right leads 1.2 mi. down to the locked Hermitage Cabin of the PATC. (Reservations to rent must be obtained in advance from PATC. See Shelters in General Information.)

Miles   Detailed Trail Data

9.6   Tumbling Run **SHELTERS** are 30 yds to the right.
        In 105 yds a blue-blazed trail leads back through
        the shelter area and in 0.6 mi. to the PATC
        Hermitage Cabin.

9.8   Reach paved Old Forge Road, turn right across
        bridge, then left into woods.

10.4   Cross Rattlesnake Run Road. A blue-blazed trail
        follows road to left for 0.2 mi., enters woods to
        right, and in another 0.2 mi. rejoins A.T. beyond
        footbridges at mileage point 10.8. This blue-blazed
        trail is a high-water route in case approaches to
        Antietam Shelter are not passable.

10.7   Reach edge of Old Forge Picnic Grounds. Frost
        free **WATER** tap is on side of well house
        immediately to right.   A.T. turns left and in 0.1
        mi. Turns right for 50 yds through a pipeline
        clearing before reentering woods.

10.8   Two footbridges for crossing East Branch of
        Antietam Creek with Antietam **SHELTER** to the
        left. If approach to the bridge area is flooded
        return to Rattlesnake Run Road and follow blue-
        blazed trail around to the other side of the
        footbridges.

12.3   Cross woods road. Rattlesnake Run Road is 0.17
        mi. to the left.

12.9   Cross a pipeline clearing. Rattlesnake Run Road is
        0.15 mi. to the left.

13.2   Pass Deer Lick **SHELTERS** and **SPRING** on the left.
        A second **SPRING** is 0.25 miles on blue-blazed trail
        from the front of the shelters.

<u>Miles</u>   <u>Detailed Trail Data</u>

14.5   Reach Bailey **SPRING** 15 yds off the trail on the
       right. It is an excellent walled spring and always
       flowing. A.T. goes left from spring for 25 yds then
       right uphill.   Use care following blazes due to
       State Forest boundary blazes and old woods roads.

14.7   Cross Rattlesnake Run Road.

15.1   Turn left on Mentzer Gap Road. In 70 yds turn
       right and reenter woods.

15.3   Trail reaches PA 16. Rouzerville is 2.1 miles west
       to the right; Blue Ridge Summit is 1.8 miles east,
       to the left. A.T. crosses PA 16, then crosses Red
       Run by a log bridge and leaves the southern
       boundary of Michaux State Forest.

15.6   Cross old PA 16. Ascend, then descend Mount
       Dunlop.

16.8   Cross Buena Vista Road, with roadside **SPRING** on
       the right. <u>Must purify water</u>. Several miles to the
       right is the site of the former Buena Vista Hotel.

17.3   Reach bench and descend sharply to footbridge
       over Falls Creek.

17.4   Pass old stone wall on right. Cross old trolley line
       road bed, which once served Pen Mar Park and
       ascend on trail.

17.7   Turn right onto power line right-of-way.

17.8   Cross Pen Mar Road.

Miles   Detailed Trail Data

17.9   Mason-Dixon Line. Enter Maryland and in 50 yds
        cross railroad tracks. A.T. then bears right in 0.2
        mi. reach center of Washington County's Pen Mar
        Park. During summer season restrooms in park are
        open. NOTE: The Mason-Dixon marker for Mile 91,
        from the 1765 survey, is on private property and is
        no longer accessible from the A.T.

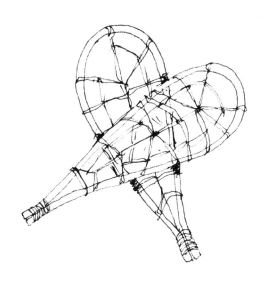

SECTION 14

PEN MAR TO CALEDONIA

SOUTH TO NORTH

Miles   Detailed Trail Data

0.0   Enter Pennsylvania. (From center of Pen Mar Park A.T. reaches state Line by descending 0.2 mi., crossing railroad tracks, and preceding another 50 yds.) NOTE: The Mason-Dixon marker for Mile 91, from the 1765 survey, is on private property and is no longer accessible from the A.T.

0.1   Cross Pen Mar Road and continue on power line right-of-way.

0.2   Turn left off right-of-way and descend into woods.

0.5   Cross old trolley line road bed which once served Pen Mar Park, descend to bridge. Pass old stone wall on left.

0.7   Cross Falls Creek on trail bridge. Ascend from bridge and turn right.

1.1   Cross Buena Vista Road. There is a roadside **SPRING** to the left. <u>Must purify water</u>. Ascend, then descend Mount Dunlop.

2.3   Cross old PA Route 16. A.T. soon crosses southern boundary of Michaux State Forest and crosses Red Run on log bridge.

Miles   Detailed Trail Data

2.6   Cross PA Route 16. Rouzerville is 2.1 miles west, to the left; Blue Ridge Summit is 1.8 miles east, to the right.

2.8   Turn left on Mentzer Gap Road. In 70 yds turn right and reenter woods.

3.2   Cross Rattlesnake Run Road.

3.4   Reach Bailey **SPRING** 15 yds off the trail on the left. It is an excellent walled spring and always running. The trail continues on right through young undergrowth.

4.7   Pass Deer Lick **SHELTERS** and **SPRING** on the right. A second **SPRING** is 0.25 miles on blue-blazed trail from the front of the shelters.

5.0   Cross a pipeline clearing. Rattlesnake Run Road is 0.15 mi. to the right.

5.6   Cross woods road.   Rattlesnake Run Road is 0.17 mi to the right.

7.1   Reach footbridges over East Branch of Antietam Creek. (If approach to bridges is flooded go back 50 yds and take the high water blue-blazed trail upstream 0.2 mi. To Rattlesnake Run Road, turn left on road and in another 0.2 mi. Reach A.T. at mileage 7.5. Follow route southbound to reach Antietam shelter.) After crossing bridge, Antietam **SHELTER** is on right. Do not drink water from the creek.   **WATER** is obtainable in the summer months from the fountains at the picnic grounds. There is a frost free tap on well house for winter use. After second bridge A.T. turns right for 50 yds through a pipeline clearing before reentering woods.

Miles   Detailed Trail Data

7.2   Reach edge of Old Forge Picnic Grounds.   A frost
           free **WATER** tap on well house immediately on left
           where trail turns right and reenters woods.

7.5   Cross Rattlesnake Run Road. Blue-blazed high
           water route described above comes in on right.

8.1   Cross Tumbling Run on Old Forge Road bridge.
           Turn left into woods.

8.3   Reach to Tumbling Run **SHELTERS** located 30 yds
           off A.T. A blue-blazed trail bearing left from the
           A.T. 0.6 mi. before the shelters leads through the
           shelter area and then in another 0.6 mi. Reach
           locked PATC Hermitage Cabin. (Reservations to
           rent must be obtained in advance from PATC. See
           Shelters in General Information.) **SPRING** is
           located across Tumbling Run about 100 yds from
           the shelters.

9.6   Near summit of Buzzard Peak reach intersection
           with a blue-blazed trail. The blue-blazed trail to the
           right leads 120 yds to Chimney Rocks, at 1,940
           feet of elevation, with a magnificent view towards
           Green Ridge and the Waynesboro Reservoir. Blue-
           blazed trail to the left leads 1.2 mile down to the
           locked PATC Hermitage Cabin.

10.4   Cross a pipeline clearing.

11.6   Cross under a power line.

12.2   Cross Snowy Mountain Road.

12.5   Cross dirt road (closed to public).

12.8   Reach Swamp Road. Turn left on road across very
           boggy area.

<u>Miles</u>   <u>Detailed Trail Data</u>

12.9   Turn right off Swamp Road.

13.0   A.T. turns left.

13.2   Cross PA 233. To the right (east) 1.6 mi. is the
        village of South Mountain with store and Post
        Office. PA 233 goes north to Caledonia Park and
        US 30. To the left, PA 233 goes to the village of
        Mont Alto, Mont Alto School of Forestry of Penn
        State University, and Mont Alto State Park.
        VisionQuest Camp entrance is visible to the right.

13.4   Cross a gravel maintenance road on ridge leading
        right 0.1 mi. to water tanks.

14.7   A.T. follows top of ridge for next 1.8 miles.

14.9   Blue-blazed side trail to the east goes 0.2 mi.
        downhill to the Rocky Mountain **SHELTERS**. This
        trail continues another 0.26 mi. To PA Rt 223.
        The **SPRING** is another 0.1 mi. south on the west
        side of PA Rt 233.

16.5   A.T. descends off ridge to west side.

17.8   Cross gas pipeline clearing.

17.9   Reach US 30. To the right (east) 0.6 mi. is PA
        233 and Caledonia State Park parking lot. Michaux
        District Forester's office is 0.4 mi. beyond. To the
        left (west) 0.9 mi. are two stores, a motel, and
        restaurant in an additional 1.6 mi.

POLE STEEPLE © Wayne E. Gross

INDEX

MEMBERSHIP APPLICATION

KEYSTONE TRAILS ASSOCIATION
PO Box 251   Cogan Station, PA 17728-0251

NAME: _____

ADDRESS: _____

_____

TELEPHONE # _____

_____

Individual Membership ($9.00)----------$ _____
Brush Cutter ($20.00)----------$ _____
Trail Blazer ($30.00)----------$ _____
Trail Builder ($50.00)----------$ _____
Life Membership (One-time payment: $225.00)--$ _____
Additional contribution----------$ _____
TOTAL ENCLOSED:----------$ _____

Check appropriate category at left and mail this form with check or money order (payable to Keystone Trails Association) to the address shown above. For Information about organizational memberships, write to KTA.

MEMBERSHIP APPLICATION

KEYSTONE TRAILS ASSOCIATION
PO Box 251   Cogan Station, PA 17728-0251

NAME: _____

ADDRESS: _____

TELEPHONE # _____

Individual Membership ($9.00)------------------ $_____
Brush Cutter ($20.00)------------------------------- $_____
Trail Blazer ($30.00)------------------------------- $_____
Trail Builder ($50.00)------------------------------ $_____
Life Membership (One-time payment: $225.00)-- $_____
Additional contribution---------------------------- $_____
TOTAL ENCLOSED:-------------------------------- $_____

Check appropriate category at left and mail this form with check or money order (payable to Keystone Trails Association) to the address shown above. For Information about organizational memberships, write to KTA.

MEMBERSHIP APPLICATION

KEYSTONE TRAILS ASSOCIATION
PO Box 251   Cogan Station, PA 17728-0251

NAME: _____

ADDRESS: _____

_____

TELEPHONE # _____

Individual Membership ($9.00)-------------- $_____
Brush Cutter ($20.00)----------------------- $_____
Trail Blazer ($30.00)------------------------ $_____
Trail Builder ($50.00)----------------------- $_____
Life Membership (One-time payment: $225.00)-- $_____
Additional contribution--------------------- $_____
TOTAL ENCLOSED:--------------------------- $_____

Check appropriate category at left and mail this form with check or money order (payable to Keystone Trails Association) to the address shown above. For Information about organizational memberships, write to KTA.

MEMBERSHIP APPLICATION

KEYSTONE TRAILS ASSOCIATION
PO Box 251   Cogan Station, PA 17728-0251

NAME: _____

ADDRESS: _____

_____

TELEPHONE # _____

Individual Membership ($9.00)-------- $_____

Brush Cutter ($20.00)-------- $_____

Trail Blazer ($30.00)-------- $_____

Trail Builder ($50.00)-------- $_____

Life Membership (One-time payment: $225.00)-- $_____

Additional contribution-------- $_____

TOTAL ENCLOSED:-------- $_____

Check appropriate category at left and mail this form with check or money order (payable to Keystone Trails Association) to the address shown above. For Information about organizational memberships, write to KTA.